GHOST TOWNS

GHOST TOWNS

Ruth E DeJauregui

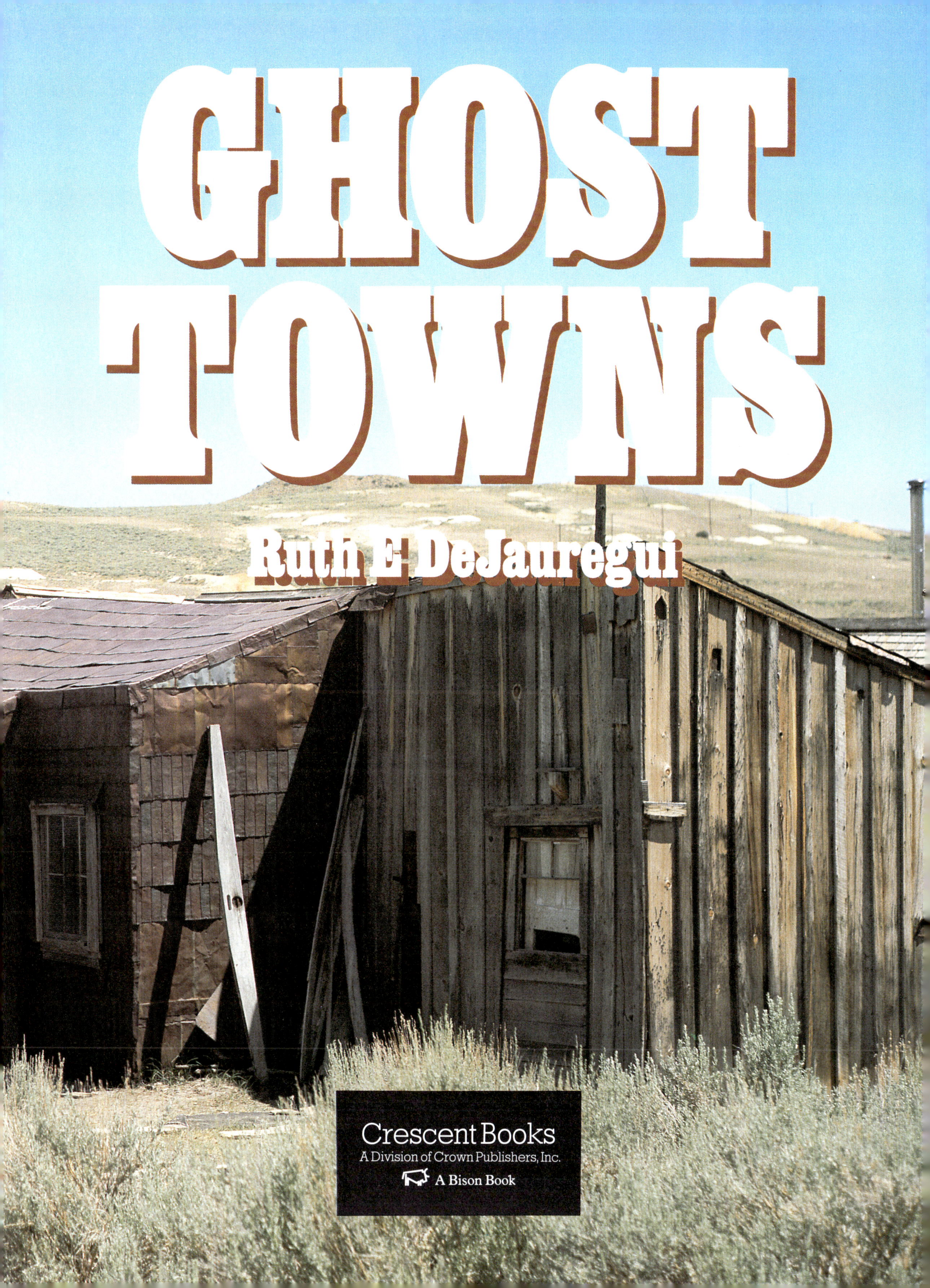

Crescent Books
A Division of Crown Publishers, Inc.
A Bison Book

The 1988 edition published by
Crescent Books, distributed by
Crown Publishers, Inc.
225 Park Avenue South
New York, NY 10003

Produced by
Bison Books Corp.
15 Sherwood Place
Greenwich, CT 06830
USA

Printed in Hong Kong

ISBN 0-517-65844-5

Designed by Ruth DeJauregui

Edited by Bill Yenne and Timothy Jacobs

Captioned by Timothy Jacobs

Page 1: **Weathered boards, broken planks and a porch fronting on high weeds are all that's left of this dwelling in Drawbridge, California. Once a scene of bustling human activity, Drawbridge—like many formerly thriving towns of the American past—is now largely the habitat of memories.**
Pages 2–3: **The western wind blows through the cracks in these old structures in Bodie, California. Chimneys made of tin, and a rusted old wash stand signify a bygone era, on the main street of a ghost town.**
These pages: **The crowd looks rough, ready and willing; most of the populace of Georgetown, California has turned out for election day in this photograph taken on 4 November 1890.**

TABLE OF CONTENTS

Introduction

Come. Walk with me for a while. Let us visit the places that our fathers knew. Let us visit the ruins that whisper stories of the past. In the mind's eye we can see the bearded prospectors, the painted ladies, the hustle and bustle of these abandoned places that men and women once called home...

All across the North American continent lie the remains of these towns, villages and mining camps. Most are completely abandoned. In some, a handful of inhabitants have lingered long after the majority of the population has moved on to greener fields. From the remnants of the Indian culture, long deteriorated into oblivion, to faint traces of Leif Erickson's Vinland settlement; from the mining camps of the West, to Love Canal in New York—from all these come the stories and the legends that make up the history of North America.

The people of the Americas have always been movers. The Indians came across the land bridge from Siberia, moving south and spreading across the lands. When the white men arrived, their superior technology allowed them to push back both the edge of the wilderness and the Indians who lived within it. Men and women built their settlements, raised their children and, when economics demanded or wanderlust struck, they moved on to new horizons. Indian attacks decimated some of the white man's towns just as European diseases had wiped out Indian settlements. Economic depression combined with gold rushes pulled men south to the Carolinas and Georgia, and finally west to California after 1849. The railroads spanned the continent, pulling men and women with them. Towns sprang up, thrived, then died when the reason for their existence left—whether it had been mines, industries or railroads.

Today, much of the folklore of these places is lost. Yet somewhere, walking through forest or meadow, mountain or plain, one can find ruins of foundations distinct among the weeds, or stone walls standing proudly in the grasses, or rotting cabins slowly collapsing in upon themselves. Much of what was built still remains, and although cities have grown up over the ruins of many old towns, some of these abandoned villages have not yet completely disappeared. Bits and pieces of the history of this continent dot the landscape, only waiting to be rediscovered by the curious. Until rediscovered by the occasional traveler, only the ghosts of memory linger in the boarded up hotels, the rusted cars, and the broken and scattered headstones of old 'Boot Hill' that rises behind the town. There lies your father, my grandmother and all those many years—drifting into legend.

Above: **The old town's inhabitants may be long gone, but many of their fellows stayed behind—up on Boot Hill, where weathered wood and wind-scoured stone mark their graves, and the old graveyard church *(at right)* stands vigil over all. *Overleaf:* One of Montana's many ghost towns—much touristed, but no longer lived in.**

HART

The New World

Columbus discovered America—as the official histories have said for hundreds of years. Rumors of Welshmen who had crossed the Atlantic have been discounted, and theories of the Egyptians trading with the Maya Indians in Mexico have been presented but no real proof has been shown to exist—at least from a scientific point of view.

Vinland, on the other hand, is an entirely different matter. The Vikings were great seamen, traveling forth from Scandanavia, they colonized many North Atlantic islands, expanding into Iceland and Greenland. The Vikings were the last of the Nordic conquerors and the first European seafaring explorers. According to the Icelandic sagas, such as the *Saga of Eric the Red* and the *Saga of the Greenlanders*, America was discovered by Bjarni Herjolfssan around the year 1000. The heroes of these tales, however, were the explorers who followed him, such as Leif Ericson (son of Eric the Red) and Thorfinn Thordarson. Both founded settlements, with Leif's being called 'Vinland' because of the wild grapes they found there. Leif and his brothers Thorstein and Thorvald explored the New World and later sagas told of a mild climate, wild wheat, tall timber and the natives who had killed Thorvald.

Vinland was abandoned for unknown reasons—and its exact location lost—but the Vikings are known to have continued to cross the Atlantic in search of timber for their ships. Many Viking artifacts have been reported along the coast of North America. A round tower in Newport, Rhode Island was supposed to have been built by the Vikings, and a stone turned up in Kensington, Minnesota which was carved with a supposed Viking inscription. The 'Kensington Stone' was, of course, a fake. Linguists found that the language was only a touched-up version of modern Swedish. Although some of the relics which have turned up appear to be authentic, many are obvious fakes like the Kensington Stone, or mistakes like the 'Viking swords' found in New England that turned out to be the broken off fragments of farm machinery.

Nonetheless, in 1963, the Norwegian explorer Helge Ingstad announced that after many years of study and investigation, a site on the northern tip of Newfoundland had revealed an authentic Scandinavian village. His excavations located at least nine structures from the Viking era, including one that measured 70 by 45 feet. There is no proof that this village near the present day L'Anse aux Meadows was actually Leif Ericson's Vinland, but the circumstantial evidence certainly points toward that conclusion.

Above: **The early European settlers crossed the ocean to America in little ships like this. After a few months of such cramped quarters, they 'made land' and built tiny but utilitarian dwellings, like the historic Kentucky cabin *at right*.**

More thoroughly documented was the disappearance of the English colonists of Roanoke Island, North Carolina. This settlement was established 22 years before John Smith and the Jamestown colonists arrived in Chesapeake Bay, and 35 years before the Mayflower set sail. In 1587 a group of men, women and children arrived at Roanoke Island. Organized by Sir Walter Raleigh and led by John White, an artist, the colony became the first permanent English settlement of the New World. Setting the proper example for his people, John White had taken his pregnant daughter with him. In this new colony Eleanor White Dare gave birth to Virginia Dare, the first child of English descent born in America.

The new colonists had not *intended* to settle on Roanoke Island; they originally had planned to establish the 'Cittie of Raleigh' on Chesapeake Bay, but their plans were changed by the sea captain that brought them to the New World, Simon Ferdinando, who ordered that

FIRST HOUSE
IN KENTUCKY

the colonists be left on the island. Fortunately, an earlier expedition had stranded 15 men on the island, and they had built some houses before disappearing. The colonists repaired these homes and began building more houses to shelter their displaced settlement. When they established contact with the Croatan Indians, they found that of the 15 men that had disappeared, two had been killed by—it was rumored—Indians of the Roanoke tribe, and the others had gotten away in a small boat.

The colonists then made a serious mistake by killing some Indians they mistakenly identified as Roanokes, who turned out to be Croatans. This situation was resolved but another question remained: Who should return to England with the ships which were soon to depart? Someone had to carry word of the colonists and bring back more supplies. The colonists determined that Governor White should go back. Governor White said no. He was stubborn, but the colonists finally prevailed. They even put it in writing, in a legal and binding document that left White no choice. To cover each point of his concerns, they wrote: '...the planters of Virginia, doe by these presents let you, and every of you to understande, that for the present and speedie supplie of certaine our knowen, and apparent lackes, and needes, most requisite and necessarie for the good and happie planting of us, or any other in this lande of Virginia, wee all of one minde, and consent, have most earnestly intreated, and uncessantly requested John White, Governour of the planters in Virginia, to passe into England, for the better and more assured helpe, and setting forward of the foresayde supplies...'

Ferdinando sent word that he was sailing on the next tide. There was no time for White to persuade anyone else to go, so he set sail for England, leaving his daughter and new granddaughter on the island. When he left, the colony held at least 110 people. He had arranged with the colonists that if the colony should be forced to move, they would carve the name of their destination on a tree or post. If danger threatened, they should then carve a Maltese cross over the lettering.

The trip back to England was horrible. Accident and disease hindered the sailors. White must have had visions of the fate awaiting his family in America because when he arrived in England, he did his best to gather the supplies and support he needed to return as quickly as possible. However, the War with Spain intervened, Sir Walter Raleigh had other things on his mind, and it was two years and seven months after White had left Roanoke that he again set sail. The ships indulged in some privateering along the way, but on 15 August 1590 White wrote: 'At our first comming to anker on this shore we saw a great smoake rise in the Ile Roanoak neere the place where I left our Colony in the yeere 1587, which smoake put us in good hope that some of the Colony were there expecting my returne out of England.'

The next day they found no sign of men at the fire near Kendricks Mount and decided to delay going on to Roanoke until the next morning. The men finally reached the spot where the colonists had been left and White's diary described what they found: 'As we entered up the sandy banke upon a tree, in the very browe thereof were curiously carved these faire Romane letters CRO: which letters presently we knew to signifie the place, where I should find the planters seated, according to a secret token agreed upon betweene them and me at my last departure from them.'

This belief was further reinforced by finding in the settlement, 'one of the chiefe trees or postes at the right side of the entrance had the bark taken off, and 5 foote from the ground in fayre Capitall letters was graven CROATAN without any crosse or signe of distress.'

With many difficulties along the way, the ship with White aboard once again arrived back in England. Though he had been unable to reach the Croatan settlement, his mind must have been somewhat at ease, believing that the settlers were safe and happy with their Croatan friends. He did not have the financing to return to America again, so the search for the colonists waited another 13 years until Sir Walter Raleigh decided to look for them. He was probably motivated by the

It is postulated that the Norseman Bjarni Herjolfssan was the first European to find America, and his countrymen Leif Erickson and Thorfinn Thordarson founded American settlements nearly *1000 years* ago. *Above* is a depiction of Thordarson's men celebrating their discovery of the New World, and *above left* are the diggings at L'Anse aux Meadows, in Newfoundland—this may be the uncovering of Ericson's settlement on 'Vinland,' and if so, this site would unquestionably be the oldest ghost town of European origin in America. *Overleaf:* From a much later time, this well-preserved ghost fort and cemetery *are* fully documented and open to visitors.

GRAVE
OF THE FIRST
WHITE CHILD
BURIED
IN KENTUCKY

expiration of his patent on Virginia; the presence of the lost colonists was necessary for continuance of that old patent. His search failed.

Not until the repeated efforts of the later Jamestown settlement and Captain John Smith was there any word of the lost colony. Smith wrote: 'At Port Cotage in our Voyage up the River, we saw a Savage Boy about the age of ten yeeres, which had a head of hairs of a perfect yellow and a reasonable white skinne, which is a Miracle amongst all Savages!'

Smith made a number of references to the lost colony in his writings. But perhaps the most startling reference came from the council at Jamestown which recorded: 'Powatan confessed that he had been at the murder of that colony, and showed a musket barrel and a brass mortar, and certain pieces of iron which had been theirs.'

It was also reported that four men, two boys and one young woman had escaped the massacre. None of these survivors were ever found. Historians often speculated that the lost colonists had survived to intermarry with the Indians, pointing out interesting legends and the presence of gray eyes among the Indians.

In the late 1800s, Hamilton McMillian set out to prove that the local tribe, the Croatans, was the result of the Indians and colonists intermarrying. He was so convinced of this fact that he carried his tale of the tribe all the way to the North Carolina General Assembly, resulting in the 1885 act to provide for separate schools for the Croatan Indians in Robeson County!

The lost colony spurred the imaginations of a number of people, resulting in the hoax of the Eleanor Dare stones. These stones were supposedly the diary of Eleanor, carved on a number of stones found in the 1930s and 1940s. Once systematically investigated, however, the stones were found to be recently carved with words that would not have been a part of Elizabethan English.

Roanoke Island had become one of the first ghost towns of the Americas. Mystery shrouded its ending and although theories abound, most were discounted, including Hamilton McMillian's claims. Certainly the colonists could have intermarried with the Indians, but other evidence points toward a massacre of most of the settlers. Roanoke was not the only settlement that became the victim of the Indians. Throughout the Americas, settlements were destroyed, though to the Indians' credit attacks were often provoked by the Europeans, and many settlements were abandoned after being ferociously attacked.

Even into the 19th century, towns were lost in this manner. Indian Keys, Florida was the site of a massacre in which only one man and his sister survived. The settlement was abandoned and the buildings fell into ruins.

While the English and French explored the east, the Spanish moved up from the south and the Russians moved down from the north along the California coast. Missions were built by Spanish priests trying to convert the Indians to Catholicism. Sometimes they succeeded and sometimes they failed. Many missions were abandoned after being attacked by Indians or after the United States took control of California. In later days many were rebuilt by the faithful.

The Russians, on the other hand, came to California to hunt for the sea otter. Outposts like Fort Ross were built to protect the hunters and to store valuable pelts. Most of these forts were left empty when the Russians withdrew from California, and only a few have been restored in recent times.

These were among the first ghost towns of North America—the settlements, forts and missions of the French, English, Spanish and Russians. Today only a few ruins, some archaeological digs and some carefully restored sites remain where the first European and Eurasian settlers tried to build their homes.

Built in 1607, Jamestown, Virginia was the first successful English settlement in America; only its foundations *(below)* now remain. *At right:* Orthodox Christian crosses adorn a chapel at Fort Ross, on the Northern California coast. This abandoned Russian fort has been restored—and the public can tour it, icons and all.

The First Gold Rush

The settling of the Americas was a long and difficult process. The disruption wrought by the Revolutionary War, the Battle of 1812, and the continual fighting with the many Indian tribes all contributed to the constant migration of the colonists and their descendants to find better places to live. Economic woes had always kept people moving, but in 1782 the imagination of the public was first fueled by the discovery of gold. Thomas Jefferson himself described the discovery of a lump weighing about four pounds on the Rappahannock River in Virginia. In 1799 more gold was discovered near Concord, North Carolina and a small Gold Rush resulted. Reed Gold Mine was quite rich, yielding one nugget that weighed 28 pounds. In 1827, the Cherokee Indians revealed the Coker Creek gold fields to white settlers, and it wasn't long before men like Jacob Peck and Le Grande Henderson were on Indian lands, busily mining. Others followed and the Cherokee complained. Soldiers were then stationed nearby to keep the white men out. The beginning of the end of the Cherokee way of life came in 1828 in Georgia when Benjamin Parks kicked over a rock and found gold 'as yellow as the yolk of an egg,' launching the first major Gold Rush in the Americas. The excitement of gold pulled men onto the Indian lands without any thought of treaties, and the Cherokee—a highly civilized people—resented the intrusion of more than 4000 prospectors on their lands.

The men who came were from every walk of life—but many were reckless men who drank, gambled and stole. One newspaper correspondent wrote in 1831: 'I can hardly conceive of a more unmoral community than exists around these mines; drunkenness, gambling, fighting, lewdness, and every other vice exist here to an awful extent. Many of the men, by working three days in the week, make several dollars, and then devote the remaining four to every species of vice.'

The Cherokee were moved west in 1838 over the 'Trail of Tears.' Tragically, it has been estimated that nearly a quarter of the Cherokee died on their way to their new homes. Some did remain behind, escaping the fate of their brothers and sisters, and became the Eastern Band of the Cherokee tribe. Obviously, the state of Georgia had very little respect for federal treaties since it divided up the Indian lands eight years before federal troops rounded up the Cherokee.

The first boom town of this Georgia phenomena, which had become known as the 'Dahlonega Gold Rush,' was Auraria. A prospector wrote in 1833: 'There is in this village 20 or 25 stores, 18 or 20 lawyers, four or five taverns, a printing office, doctors, barbers, billiard tables, etcetera, and in all making about 1000 inhabitants. A third of which must starve this summer...I do really believe that for a man to be thought honest here, would be a disadvantage to him, or at least he would be set down for a fool and treated accordingly.'

At right: **A bust portrait of Sequoyah, a chief of the Cherokee at the time of the Dahlonega Gold Rush.** ***Above:*** **Benjamin Parks—who started the Dahlonega Gold Rush—looking like the harbinger of doom for the Cherokee of Georgia.**

First known as Nuckollsville or Knucklesville, Auraria was a place where most men were content to settle their differences with their fists rather than resorting to gunfights as in Western towns. The town didn't last long. When Dahlonega was named the county seat of Georgia's then-newly formed Lumpkin County, Auraria's population slowly dwindled. While Dahlonega never became a ghost town, the surrounding area was filled with the relics and history of the Georgia gold boom.

At least 35 million dollars' worth of gold was found in Georgia, but in 1849 the news of the California gold strike reached the ears of Georgia's eager prospectors. One day, as about 200 miners gathered, preparing to move to California, the assayer of Lumpkin County, Dr Matthew F Stephenson, stood on the balcony of the court house and pleaded with the men.

'Why go to California? *There's gold in them thar hills.* In that ridge lies more gold than many ever dreamed of. There's millions in it!'

The Georgia miners repeated Stephenson's phrase throughout California and Mark Twain picked up the quote and put it into the mouth of his character, Colonel Mulberry Sellers, in 'The Gilded Age.'

One would think that the miners would have remembered what had happened at the Battle Branch Mine on the Etowah River. Named for a bloody battle in 1831 between Georgia and Tennessee miners, the mine eventually came to be owned by Major John Hockenhull, who later faced closure of the mine in 1843. He called his workers together and explained that there was no more money, leaving the decision to them whether they should stay or leave. Only one man, John Pasco, volunteered to help the Major. After the others had left, Major Hockenhull and John Pasco went to work. A few minutes later they uncovered a pocket of gold. The discovery of more gold pockets followed, and over $80,000 was taken from the mine.

The prospectors, however, inflamed by the wild rumors from California, forgot all such past experiences in their lust for the rumored fabulous amounts of California gold. Hundreds of men and boys headed westward, where their previous work experience in the gold fields of Georgia would serve many of them well.

Not all of the miners went west. There were many who continued to work in the Georgia mines, which helped to keep open the US mint in Dahlonega: up until the Civil War, it coined more than six million dollars in gold coins. When Georgia seceded from the Union, the mint closed, leading one prominent citizen, Harrison W Riley, to threaten to seize the mint. He claimed that the money did not belong any one person and that he was as entitled to it as anyone else. The employees of the mint thwarted his plans by arming themselves and making it clear that they would not tolerate any theft from 'their' mint.

Below left: **Barlow Cut, Lumpkin County, Georgia, where much Dahlonega mining took place.** ***Above:*** **Lumpkin County Assayer Dr Matthew Stephenson, who originated the statement, 'There's gold in them thar hills.'** ***Above right:*** **The Graham Hotel, in Auraria—which died with the Dahlonega Gold Rush.** ***Below right:*** **Workings at the Calhoun Mine, in 1940.** ***Below far right:*** **A Gold Rush-era gravestone.**

Some miners returned to Georgia before the Civil War broke out, attempting some small hydraulic operations, but it wasn't until after the war ended that large-scale operations resumed. Gold mining continued under corporate ownership until the World War II, but since then, there haven't been any large-scale operations. The last big find in Georgia was in 1938, when the entrance to the Calhoun Mine (which had belonged to Georgia's pioneer prospector, Benjamin Parks), was being enlarged: gold was discovered less than two feet below the path that miners had traveled for more than 100 years!

Like Georgia, North Carolina also had its gold towns. It was the location for a gold 'strike' in the 1860s. The Civil War interrupted the miners' work, which resumed around Albemarle, NC, but the town faded away in the early 1900s. Albemarle eventually revived to become an agricultural and industrial center.

The miners of Georgia played a significant part in the California Gold Rush. Without the experience they had gained back in their home state, many gold fields would have remained unrecognized and unknown. Although some returned to Georgia, most remained in the West, following the trail of gold wherever it led them, from California to Oregon to Colorado to the Yukon. Some found their golden dream. Some did not. Whether or not the riches they found brought them happiness is a moot point. For many, it did not, and historically *has* not. Surely many of the prospectors came to realize that fact in California.

AGNES
PASCHAL,
BORN
June 11, 1776
DIED
Oct. 23, 1869

Gold in the California Hills

It was in the spring of 1848 when Sam Brannan strode the streets of San Francisco shouting, 'Gold! Gold! Gold from the American River!'

With each telling the legend of the California Gold Rush grew. It is true that men abandoned their stores, their jobs and even their families for the lure of instant riches at Sutter's Mill.

However, 1848 had not been the first discovery of gold in California. Russian trappers spoke of mining operations at Fort Ross and Bodega Bay as early as 1814, and four years later there was a claim staked on the Feather River. California has always been filled with wild tales of gold, from the secret mines of the Jesuits, to the madness of the Gold Rush days, to the legends of the lost mines that persist even to the present.

According to available records, however, it was Francisco Lopez, a vaquero on the rancho of Ignacio del Valle, who first discovered gold at Placerita Canyon in the San Fernando Valley on 1 March 1842. While he and two friends were resting on a hillside during a search for stray cattle, he idly dug up some wild onion. Noticing the glittering soil clinging to the roots, the men decided the metal was probably copper. Lopez gathered some of the soil to show his friends at the cantina. When he displayed his find, they excitedly pronounced it to be gold and the group returned to the onion bed. There the Sonorans scraped up some soil with a horn spoon and washed it in the creek. With the residue of gold flakes, they spread the good news to friends on the neighboring ranches. At the San Fernando 'placers,' or gold washes, unlike at the later gold camps, strict order prevailed. The owner of the ranch, Don Sebastian del Valle, was appointed as the magistrate and a man named Zorillo in effect became his sheriff. They kept order, levied dues on liquor sales, portioned out land, imposed taxes and collected fees for wood, pasture and mineral privileges. Even at its peak, the San Fernando placer only produced 2000 ounces of gold. Gradually, the mine was stripped and eventually forgotten.

Six years later, in 1848, however, James Marshall made the discovery at a place called Sutter's Mill that would change the entire western half of the continent.

Captain John August Sutter, born in Germany of Swiss parents, had wandered through the west, arriving in California by way of what are now known as Indiana, New Mexico, Oregon, Hawaii and Alaska. Sutter took out Mexican citizenship in 1840, and by 1841 had received a land grant of 76 square miles. He convinced the Mexican authorities

Above: **This dapper old fellow was photographed in 1931; he points to the place where Francisco Lopez discovered the first gold in the San Fernando Valley in 1842.** ***At right:*** **The James Marshall Monument in Coloma, California; Marshall discovered gold at Sutter's Mill, and inadvertently touched off the California Gold Rush.**

that he could build a viable farming community that would serve the northern half of the state. Building his fort near the confluence of the American and Sacramento Rivers, he named his community New Helvetia. He ran a trading post and operated his farms and ranches, becoming a wealthy businessman whose little empire survived almost untouched by the upheavals in the Mexican government, the short-lived 'Bear Flag' rebellion and the eventual takeover by the United States in June 1846. Sutter's downfall would be his own drive and ambition. He already had several flour mills serving his community but he decided that a reliable source of lumber was needed, so he hired James Marshall to build a sawmill on the American River. Sutter and Marshall felt that they could sell the excess lumber in Yerba Buena (which later became San Francisco). Marshall later wrote of the days before his momentous discovery:

'In May 1847, with my rifle, blanket, and a few crackers to eat with the venison—for the deer then was awful plenty—I ascended the American River, according to Mr Sutter's wish, as he wanted to find a good site for a sawmill, where we could have plenty of timber, and where the wagons would be able to ascend and descend the river hills. Many fellows had been out before me, but they could not find any place to suit; so when I left I told Mr Sutter I would go along the river to the very head and find the place, if such a place existed anywhere upon the river or any of its forks. I traveled along the river the whole way. Many places would suit very well for the erection of the mill, with plenty of timber everywhere, but then nothing but a mule could climb the hills; and when I would find a spot where the hills were not steep, there was no timber to be had; and so it was until I had been out several days and reached this place, which, at first sight, looked like the exact spot we were hunting.

'I passed a couple of days examining the hills, and found a place where wagons could ascend and descend with all ease. On my return to the fort I went out through the country examining the canyons and gulches, and picking out the easiest places for crossing them with loaded wagons.

'You may be sure Mr Sutter was pleased when I reported my success. We entered into partnership; I was to build the mill, and he was to find provisions, teams, tools and to pay a portion of the men's wages. I believe I was at the time the only millwright in the whole country. In August, everything being ready, we freighted two wagons with tools and provisions, and accompanied by six men I left the fort, and after a good deal of difficulty, reached this place one beautiful afternoon and formed our camp on yon little rise of ground right above the town (Coloma).

'Our first business was to put up log houses, as we intended remaining here all winter. This was done in less than no time, for my men were great with the axe. We then cut timber and fell to work hewing it for the framework of the mill. The Indians gathered about us in great numbers. I employed about 40 of them to assist us with the dam, which we put up in a kind of way in about four weeks. In digging the foundation of the mill, we cut some distance into the soft granite. We opened the foreby and then I left for the fort, giving orders to Mr Weimar to have a ditch cut through the bar in the rear of the mill, and after quitting work in the evening to raise the gate and let the water run all night; as it would assist us very much in deepening and widening the mill race.

'I returned in a few days and found everything favorable, all the men being at work in the ditch. When the channel was opened it was my custom every evening to raise the gate and let the water wash out as much sand and gravel through the night as possible; and in the morning, while the men were getting breakfast, I would walk down, and, shutting off the water, look along the race and see what was to be done, so that I might tell Mr Weimar, who had charge of the Indians, at what particular point to set them to work for the day. As I was the only millwright present, all my time was employed upon the frame work and machinery.

'One morning in January, it was a clear cold morning; I shall never forget that morning, as I was taking my usual walk along the race, after shutting off the water, my eye was caught by a glimpse of something shining in the bottom of the ditch. There was about a foot of water running there. I reached my hand down and picked it up; it made my heart thump for I felt certain it was gold. The piece was about half the size and shape of a pea. Then I saw another piece in the water. After taking it out, I sat down and began to think right hard. I thought it was gold, and yet it did not seem to be of the right color; all the gold coin I had seen

was of a reddish tinge; this looked more like brass. I recalled to mind all the metals I had ever seen or heard of, but I could find none that resembled this. Suddenly the idea flashed across my mind that it might be iron pyrites. I trembled to think of it! This question could soon be determined. Putting one of the pieces on hard river stone, I took another and commenced hammering it. It was soft and didn't break; it therefore must be gold, but largely mixed with some other metal, very likely silver; for pure gold, I thought, would certainly have a brighter color.

'When I returned to our cabin for breakfast I showed the two pieces to my men. They were all a good deal excited, and had they not thought that the gold only existed in small quantities they would have abandoned everything and left me to finish the job alone. However, to satisfy them, I told them that as soon as we had the mill finished we would devote a week or two to gold hunting and see what we could make out of it.

'While we were working in the race after this discovery, we always kept a sharp lookout, and in the course of three or four days we had picked up about three ounces—our work still progressing as lively as ever, for none of us imagined at that time that the whole country was sowed with gold.

'About a week's time after the discovery I had to take another trip to the fort; and to gain what information I could respecting the real value of the metal, took all we had collected with me and showed it to Mr Sutter, who at once declared it was gold, but thought with me, it was greatly mixed with some other metal. It puzzled us a great deal to hit upon the means of telling the exact quantity contained in the alloy; however, we at last stumbled on an old American cyclopedia where we saw the specific gravity of all the metals, and rules given to find the quantity of each in a given bulk. After hunting over the whole fort and borrowing from some of the men, we got three dollars and a half in silver, and with a small pair of scales we soon cyphered it out that there was no silver nor copper in the gold, but that it was entirely pure.

'This fact being ascertained, we thought it our best policy to keep it as quiet as possible till we should have finished our mill, but there was a great number of disbanded Mormon soldiers in and about the fort, and when they came to hear of it, why it just spread like wildfire, and soon the whole country was in a bustle. I had scarcely arrived at the mill again till several persons appeared with pans, shovels and hoes, and those that had not iron picks had wooden ones, all anxious to fall to work and dig up our mill; but this we would not permit. As fast as one party disappeared another would arrive, and sometimes I had the greatest kind of trouble to get rid of them. I sent them off in different directions, telling them about such and such places, where I was certain there was plenty of gold if they would only take the trouble of looking for it. At that time I never imagined the gold was so abundant. I told them to go to such and such places, because it appeared that they would dig nowhere but in such places as I pointed out, and I believe such was their confidence in me that they would have dug on the very top of yon mountain if I had told them to do so.'

***Below opposite:* The American River, near the 'Sutter's Mill' gold strike site. *Below:* Panning gold by Sutter's Mill. *Bottom:* A mining company marker in the American River. *Overleaf:* Some of James Marshall's contemporaries and fellow miners, left to right: Henry Bigler, William Johnson, Azariah Smith and James Brown.**

There has been some debate as to exactly what day Marshall found the gold. In later years Marshall, Mrs Wimmer (the cook), Henry Bigler and James Brown each tried to place the discovery date. Bigler said it was the 24th; Brown said it was the 23rd. Another workman, Azariah Smith, noted on 30 January in his diary that Marshall had found gold that week and had gone to the fort. At one point, Mrs Wimmer even insisted that one of her sons had made the first discovery, and that Marshall heard about it from her husband. Today it is generally accepted that James Marshall first found gold on 24 January 1848. Some of the confusion about the actual date is due to the fact that Marshall himself, in later years, wrote and rewrote his accounts of the initial discovery many times.

Having made his discovery Marshall set out for Sutter's Fort and, according to Sutter's diary: 'It was a rainy afternoon when Mr Marshall arrived at my office in the Fort, very wet....He told me then that he had some important and interesting news which he wished to communicate secretly to me, and wished me to go with him to a place where we should not be disturbed, and where no listeners could come and hear what we had to say.'

Sutter and Marshall retired to a small room and then: 'Just at the moment when Marshall took a rag from his pocket, showing me the yellow metal: he had about two ounces of it; but how quick Mr M put the yellow metal in his pocket again can hardly be described. The clerk came to see me on business, and excused himself for interrupting me, and as soon as he had left I was told, "now lock the doors; didn't I tell you that we might have listeners?"...Then Mr M began to show me this metal, which consisted of small pieces and specimens, some of them worth a few dollars; he told me that he had expressed his opinion to the laborers at the mill, that this might be gold; but some of them were laughing at him and called him a crazy man, and could not believe such a thing.'

After Sutter was convinced, they agreed to keep the secret for six weeks, enough time to finish the sawmill and the flour mill. Unfortunately for Sutter the discovery site was not part of his original grant, so one of the mill hands, Charles Bennett, was sworn to secrecy and sent to the military governor, Col Richard B Mason. Bennett carried gold specimens and a letter asking for a pre-emption on the quarter section of land around the sawmill. Sutter's greatest mistake was in sending Bennett; the news was so exciting that Bennett announced it at an overnight stop in Benicia at the mouth of the Sacramento River at the north end of San Francisco Bay. He just couldn't resist when he met some men who were excitedly discussing a coal mine near Mt Diablo.

'Coal? I'll show you some coal—the kind they mine on the American River,' he scoffed, as he pulled out a buckskin bag filled with six ounces of gold dust. He then spilled out the whole story. He blabbed again, in San Francisco, where he displayed the gold before continuing on to his rendezvous with the governor in Monterey. By the time he stamped into Mason's office to present the gold and the letter, the rumors of gold were trickling out of the Sierra.

Meanwhile, Sutter's sawmill needed supplies, so he sent a wagon up the river. When the teamster, Jacob Whittmer, returned to Sutter's Fort he brought back a sack of gold dust. The secret was out. The Mormon workmen at the sawmill had already been prospecting on the Sabbath, their only free day, and soon more workers were abandoning the Fort and heading upriver. On 7 March, Sutter wrote, in his novel grammatical style: 'The first party of Mormons, employed by me left for washing and digging Gold and very soon all followed, and left me only the sick and the lame behind. And at this time I could say that everybody left me from the Clerk to the Cook. What great Damages I had to suffer in my tannery which was just doing a profitable and extensive business, and the Vats was left filled and a quantity of half finished leather was spoiled, likewise a large quantity of raw hides collected by the farmers and of my own killing. The same thing was in every branch of business which I carried on at the time. I began to harvest my wheat, while others was digging and washing Gold, but even the Indians could not be keeped longer at Work. They was impatient to run to the mines, and other Indians had informed them of the Gold and its Value: and so I had to leave more than two-thirds of my harvest in the fields.'

Above: **Colonel Richard B Mason, military governor of California at the time of the California Gold Rush. John Sutter's emissary to the Governor couldn't keep a secret, and the news of the gold at Sutter's Mill spread like wildfire.** ***Above right:*** **A modern-day 'miner' uses the technique of washing gold from stream sediment.**

Those Mormons—Henry Bigler, Sidney Wills, William Hudson, Azariah Smith and Levi Fifield—explored upriver, finding even more gold and laying their claims. Others trailed after them and founded the first gold camp of the great California Gold Rush, Mormon Bar. Sam Brannan came, surveyed the busy scenes at the sawmill and Mormon Bar, Mormon Island and Mormon Diggings, and imagined the flood of business that the Gold Rush would bring. A merchant and trader, Brannan sold everything from blankets to shovels to whiskey. By mid-May he was back in San Francisco spreading the word of vast riches just waiting to be gathered up by those with ambition.

Suddenly, the Gold Rush was on. Soldiers deserted their posts, men abandoned their work and San Francisco became a town of women and children. The prospectors swooped down on Sutter's Fort like locusts and when Sutter had no more supplies to sell, they stole everything—even the hinges on his doors and gates. Hundreds more were on their way. From San Jose, the jailer rushed to the gold fields, bringing his prisoners with him. San Francisco's first schoolteacher, the two newspaper editors, the carpenters, clerks and clergymen all joined in the exodus. On 20 June, a messenger pounded back into Monterey. Sent to verify the rumors, he passed around nuggets he'd brought back from the mines, and Monterey was thrown into a panic. One boarding

housekeeper was reported to have even run off without collecting her lodgers' bills! By July the news had reached Los Angeles and the result was the same. Everyone headed for the American River.

The news had flown beyond California as early as June. Returning members of the Mormon Battalion, veterans of the Mexican War, brought the news to Salt Lake City, where Brigham Young thundered, 'If you elders of Israel want to go to the gold mines, then go and be damned.'

Only a few Mormons hitched up and hurried to California as Young roared, 'If they have a golden god in their hearts they had better stay where they are.' Even Bigler and his men turned away from the gold fields and went home to Salt Lake. Still, the news was slowly spreading. On 29 August 1848 the New York Journal of Commerce printed this letter from a Monterey correspondent: 'At present, people are running over the country and picking it (gold) out of the earth here and there just like a thousand hogs let loose in a forest would root up ground nuts. Some get eight or 10 ounces a day and the least active one or two. They make most who employ the wild Indians to hunt it for them. There is one man who has 60 Indians in his employ; his profits are a dollar a minute. The wild Indians know nothing of its value and wonder what the palefaces want to do with it; and they will give an ounce of it for the same weight of coined silver or a thimbleful of glass beads; or a glass of grog. And white men themselves often give an ounce of it, which is worth at our mint 18 dollars or more, for a bottle of brandy or a bottle of soda-powders or a plug of tobacco.'

From Oregon to Peru, the entire western rim of the continent was inflamed with gold fever. When samples of the gold arrived by special courier in Washington, President Polk went before Congress on 5 December 1848 and declared: 'It was known that mines of the precious metals existed to a considerable extent in California at the time of its acquisition. Recent discoveries render it probable that these mines are more extensive and valuable than was anticipated. The accounts of the abundance of gold in that territory are of such an extraordinary character as would scarcely command belief, were they not corroborated by the authentic reports of officers in the public service, who have visited the mineral district, and derived the facts which they detail from personal observation.'

While the rest of the country was only beginning to believe the fantastic tales emerging from California, the boom towns were already springing up. The first areas to attract Sutter's men—Mormon Bar, Mormon Island and Mormon Diggings—were only the beginning. John Bidwell visited Coloma in early April, carefully noting the use of the gold pan and the rocker (a cradle for panning ore) and observing the type of soil that was being worked. Remembering similar soils near his home in Chico, he returned home and prospected along the Feather River with his Indian helpers; and Bidwell's Bar was born. PB Reading was also convinced that his ranch in the upper Sacramento Valley hid gold. He and his hired Indians began mining along Clear Creek.

Along the middle fork of the American River, the Mormon miners were the pioneers: John Sinclair mined where the forks unite; William Daylor began mining at Dry Diggings, which later became Hangtown (then Placerville); Potter's Bar and Adamstown on the Feather River were founded by John Potter and Samuel Neale, while the valley of the Yuba River was mined by Jacob Leese and his associates from Sonoma.

All along the Feather, the Yuba, the American and the Bear rivers these pioneer miners found gold. Some, like Isaac Humphrey, were veterans of the earlier Gold Rushes in Tennessee, Georgia and North Carolina. In fact (although many legends credit an unknown miner with an Indian basket) Isaac Humphrey was the man who introduced the gold pan to California at Coloma. He had also been the first to use the rocker in California, probably in April 1848.

Many other devices were used to remove the gold from the river gravel, though few came to symbolize the process more than the gold pan. It would be partly filled with gravel and dirt, which was in turn washed in the river. The gold, being heavier, sank to the bottom, as the rocks and dirt were swirled out. Like the gold pan, the rocker was known long before the California Gold Rush. Faster than panning, the rocker was a large trough having cleats across its lower end, and a handle to allow the miner to 'rock' the trough. Gravel was shoveled into the upper end where a hopper sorted out the larger rocks. Water was then bailed in, flushing the gravel toward the open lower end of the rocker. The gold was caught by the cleats as the debris was washed out. A lot of gold was lost by this method, but it was very fast and became immediately popular.

Henry Bigler, who left the diggings, said that he and James Brown had tried bed-sheet mining. They spread a sheet on sloping ground, shoveled gravel over it, then splashed water onto the sheet until only the gold remained. Some miners also tried 'dry' washing. They tossed the soil into the air, trusting that the wind would blow away the dirt, leaving gold behind. Many miners preferred using a knife to pry the gold from the riverbeds: Gold was so easily available that no more than a pan and a knife were needed.

Men were stumbling over fortunes. One struck a three ounce nugget while digging a tent pole. Another rolled over a rock he'd been sitting on and found half a pound of gold. But in 1848 the wages of prospecting were still low and the necessities of life were more expensive by the day. Blankets were $50 to $100 each. Butter went as high as $6 a pound. Sam Brannan and the other merchants were realizing their dreams of riches long before the prospectors, and the Gold Rush had only begun! By the end of 1848, there were still no more than eight or 10 thousand prospectors at the diggings—their numbers had thinned somewhat because of illnesses during the heat of summer. As the rainy season approached, many went to spend the winter months in Sacramento. The winters of Northern California's gold country were very harsh, and the prudent man retreated from the mountains. General Vallejo wrote:

'There were undoubtedly many cases of miners, owners of rich placers, who feared to lose their claims if they abandoned them during the winter, and so remained in the diggings during the rainy season. Some of these men lost their lives, buried under the snow, some were drowned in the rivers and some were devoured by wild beasts. Misfortunes of this sort were very frequent in the district behind Downieville, where in the winter the snow lies to a depth of eight, 10 or 12 feet, and wild animals are abundant.

'In the winter, Sacramento was crowded, and it was there that the gamblers assembled in droves to fleece the unwary. Gaming tables were set up everywhere and faro, monte, rouge et noire and lasquinet were favorite games. The amounts wagered on a single card were very great, and there were times when they reached five or six hundred ounces of gold.'

Below: **This big old wagon symbolizes the main means by which families and supplies were carried from East to West during the Gold Rush.** ***Above Opposite:*** **A marker on the Oregon Trail.** ***Below right:*** **Nebraskans re-enact the days of the wagon trains.**

Surrounded by this extravagance, John Sutter first rented stalls and shops in his fort to merchants, barkeepers and a hotelman, but the situation was so frantic that Sutter himself was driven out of his fort.

The day after the President's endorsement of the Gold Rush in December 1848, gold hunters sailed from Boston, bound for San Francisco by way of Cape Horn. Others, not wanting to endure the long voyage around the tip of South America, went to Panama, hoping to catch a ship on the Pacific side of the Isthmus. Those who couldn't afford the sea fare gathered together and set out overland in 'prairie schooners'—covered wagons. Newspaperman Bayard Taylor wrote:

'The great starting point for this route was Independence, Missouri where thousands were encamped through the month of April, waiting until the grass should be sufficiently high for their cattle, before they ventured on the broad ocean of the Plains. From the first of May to the first of June, company after company took its departure from the frontier of civilization, til the emigrant trail....was one long line of mule-trains and wagons.'

Unlike the sea routes, the overland routes did not require large outlays of cash. A farmer could easily convert his equipment into a trail outfit. A wagon, a farm team, an axe and a gun, and all the home-grown staples of flour, meal and bacon were already available. Some took their families but many planned to make their fortunes and head back home. Still, many of the good-byes were final. The trails were long and the unknown lay ahead.

Whether the wagons followed the Oregon, the Mormon, the Lewis and Clark or any of the other trails, the story was the same. The trail was littered with excess baggage. All the luxuries went first. Then the provisions and even firearms were abandoned. Most lightened their loads too late. Dead oxen and mules lay bloated in the sun. William G

Johnston, a member of the first wagon train to reach California, wrote of the difficulties of the trail.

'June 10th. Following up the Sweetwater we encountered chilling showers of hail and rain, and in the ravines lay considerable fields of snow. In spite of heavy clothing we were nearly frozen. In the afternoon it became even worse, for every man was clad in an armor of ice; the mules too were harnessed in ice and each wagon cover had ice for an outer covering. Such was the condition when at three o'clock we reached the South Pass of the Rocky Mountains. At the time, I was driving a wagon belonging to Stewart's mess, for the regular driver was so benumbed by the fierce storm that he could no longer hold the reins. The approach to this elevation is so gradual that its culminating point would not be noticed by the ordinary traveler, had not all the surroundings been carefully noted by Fremont. Watching for the landmarks, I turned about in my saddle, took a farewell look in the direction from which we had come, conscious of having reached the dividing line between east and west. Almost two miles farther on, we came to Pacific Spring, the first water that empties into the Pacific Ocean....

'June 21st. The real troubles of mountain climbing began with this day. From Weber River the road led over a succession of elevations and our struggles were without cessation. The trail led up a ravine, narrow and precipitious, down which coursed a stream of no great proportions but sufficient to occasion difficulties which at times seemed impossible to overcome. The mire in places was of ascertained depth, in others it appeared fathomless. Occasionally the river was confined to a narrow space, but again it overspread the entire pass and it had washed out the earth and left bare rocks and boulders which clogged our way over which mules and wagon wheels had to be pulled or lifted constantly. Thus in labors inconceivable and altogether indescribable we toiled up the well nigh inaccessible heights of the Wasatch range while the day wore on and night found both men and beasts weary and exhausted. Our night camp was in the ravine, on either side hemmed in by precipitous walls. Up these walls, while the evening meal was in preparation, all the men not so engaged scrambled to points on the mountainside where with common case knives they cut grass and carried it to the mules below....'

Johnston wrote further of their travels and experiences, and the hardship of the trail was so accepted that even his diary made no complaints about their difficulties. They passed through Salt Lake City, where Johnson spoke much of the beauty of the Mormon women. (Although his judgement may have been influenced by the two months he had been on the trail.) After Salt Lake they faced the desert.

'July 16th. At four we were jogging along. The early air was pleasant but by nine o'clock the sun blazed fiercely upon us. Brinish as it was, we drank water gratefully from our canteens. Then discovery was made that, by a terrible blunder, every cask was empty. The mules had been watered before starting but by some mistake no water was brought for the men during the day.

'At every step we sank in the deep sand and were compelled often to seek rest by sitting down on the desolate wayside. For the few grains of comfort to be derived from a contact with less heated layers of sand beneath, we brushed aside those that overspread the surface and tried to imagine we were then made cooler.

'As if in cruel mockery to torture us while already suffering sufficiently, again and again mirages arose, deceiving with pleasing enchantments.

'About midday a wind began to sweep across the arid waste like a blast vomited from a Stygian furnace. At two o'clock we reached the Carson River and many leaped down the steep banks into the rushing current, drinking an amount of water which would seem incredible. After a rest of a couple of hours we continued our journey....

'July 24th. A short way from camp we realized that we no longer had mountains to climb. Our route lay over the foothills at the western base of the Sierra. We had reached California, the first train with wagons to enter California. Our journey had reached its consummation, having been accomplished in 88 days, a total of nineteen hundred and seventy-four miles.'

Johnston's group was fortunate. They had a good guide and, being among the first wagon trains to leave, they had pasture for the animals along at least part of the way. Later groups had to forage far from the trail for pasture, firewood and game. Cholera haunted the trails. Bayard Taylor wrote: 'It is estimated that about 4000 persons perished from this cause. Men were seized without warning with the most violent symptoms, and instances occurred in which the sufferer was left to die alone by the roadside, while his panic-stricken companions pushed forward, vainly trusting to get beyond the influence of the epidemic.'

Graves lined the overland routes. Yet no road was easy. The sea routes were much more expensive. When the ships sailed and the storm winds and waves lashed at the sails, no doubt many of the eager 49ers wished they had gone to California by land instead of sea.

Between the raging storms of the Cape, the disease ridden ports of Panama, the hazards of the overland trek and the impatience of the pas-

sengers, it was a wonder that so many reached California alive. Still, at every port, the latest rumor of the riches of gold and yet more gold helped to spur the ships on. By the time the ships reached San Francisco both passengers and crews abandoned the vessels, leaving the hulks to be stripped and then to rot in the Bay. It was a lucky captain who managed to keep enough crew to sail out again.

The mad rush for gold continued up the river to Sacramento. If the prospectors could not buy passage on a river boat, they had to travel by wagon or pack mules. Often bogged down in the mudflats of Suisun Bay, the stories of the mosquito attacks grew with every telling. They were reported to be so thick that the only way to eat a meal was to climb the rigging to get above the mosquitos; so big that a hat that blew off would hang in the air, held up by the giant mosquitos.

Finally, after the long months of travel, the 49ers reached Sacramento. Here was civilization. Of those who survived, some never made it to the gold country around Sutter's Mill—they struck gold on the Feather and Yuba Rivers as they crossed into California's gold fields. Soon the great rush of 1849 was over, but the days of the boom towns had only begun.

At right: A modern-day vignette of life on the trail in the days of the wagon trains to California—where you could follow the Gold Rush by water. _Below_ is an 1866 photograph of the Sacramento River steamer _Amelia_ at the wharf in San Francisco.

James Marshall

During that first summer of 1848, there was so much gold that the prospectors treated it almost as if the supply would never end. No matter how flamboyant, the tales of California's wealth named places and people, further enflaming the lust for gold. Chasing a runaway cow, a man stubbed his toe and found a fortune. Three Frenchmen dug $5000 out of a hole when they uprooted a tree stump from the middle of the Coloma road. For Captain Sutter and James Marshall the Gold Rush was the bitter end to all their dreams. Marshall was forced to put out armed guards to protect his claims at Coloma. Prospectors swarmed everywhere and when they overran Marshall's lands and began building the town of Coloma, he tried to appeal to the courts. Friends of the trespassers filled the jury box and so Marshall was cheated by both the miners and by his own lawyers, who were hoping to make a better deal with the claim jumpers. He eventually gave up his claim but many believed in his 'magic touch' and harrassed him wherever he went.

When poor Marshall began mining, the hangers on immediately surrounded the area and again and again overran Marshall's claims. There was so much gold, however, that wherever Marshall tried to send the miners to get rid of them, they found even more gold, thus enhancing his reputation. He even tried to get rid of one persistent Australian prospector by telling him to go back home. That miner did just what Marshall told him to, going back home and setting off the Australian Gold Rush. Marshall moved from place to place, trying to cash in on his discovery, first by mining, then by lecturing, but all his efforts failed. For about two years he did receive a pension from the legislature. A San Francisco reporter had taken up his cause and aroused public opinion but the public was fickle and by 1874 the pension was cut in half. James Marshall died a pauper on 10 August 1885 and was buried on a hill overlooking his discovery site. In 1890 the Native Sons of the Golden West erected a monument over his grave, pointing down the hill toward the ruins of the old mill.

Below: James Marshall's cabin. Because he made the discovery that touched off the Gold Rush, he was harassed from claim to claim by greedy claim-jumpers, and died a pauper. _Above:_ Sacramento, California in 1849. _Below right:_ The old 'Chinese Store,' in Coloma, evidences the considerable presence of Chinese miners in the Gold Rush.

Captain John Sutter

Captain John Sutter was also plagued by the eager gold seekers. Whatever they could not buy, they would steal and eventually Sutter and his men were forced to leave the fort.

Sutter was among those who went to Volcano in the spring of 1849. Attempting some mining with the help of Indians and South Sea Islanders, he was quickly accused of using 'slave labor.' Sutter and his men were forced to leave under threat of a noose. Ten miles west of Volcano lay Sutter Creek. Here Sutter and his men again tried to rebuild Sutter's lost fortunes but Sutter again was run out by the cries of 'slave labor.' He himself eventually wrote that 'I located the camp on Sutter Creek, and thought I should be there alone. The work was going on well for a while, until three or four traveling grog shops surrounded me. Then, of course, the gold was taken to these places for drinking, gambling, and etc, and the following day they were sick and unable to work. I found that it was high time to quit this kind of business and lose no more time and money. This whole expedition proved to be a heavy loss to me.'

Although Sutter himself did not mention it, the American miners could not accept his old fashioned ways of handling his laborers. Eventually Sutter withdrew to another ranch and gradually sold off his remaining lands to pay for his lawyers. When his house burned down in 1865 he fled California, moving to Washington DC, then to Pennsylvania. He did receive a small pension from Congress but his claim for the properties he had lost was never granted. On 16 June 1880 Congress again considered Sutter's petition and, for the 16th time, no action was taken. Two days later Sutter died. Wearing a ring made from the first gold found in the American River, his life ended bitterly, alone and penniless in a Washington hotel.

Coloma

The town that grew up around Sutter's Mill was the first white settlement in the Sierra foothills, the focal point of the 'Mother Lode' country which stretched 150 miles along the western slopes of the Sierras. The northernmost end of the Mother Lode extends into Plumas County while the southern end is considered to be the ghost town of Morman Bar (not to be confused with the Mormon Bar on the American River above Coloma). Coloma was where the mining town tradition of outrageous prices began. Described as a place of marked cards, loaded dice and false weights, Coloma was actually one of the quieter mining towns. In the early days of the Gold Rush entertainment was so rare that the auction of a pair of boots, a blanket or mining equipment was a festive occasion.

Hangings were common but few had the brass bands and spirit of festival that prevailed in other Sierra mining towns. In 1855, Coloma held a double hanging. One of the accused was a teacher who had killed a young woman who had rejected him. The other was an ordinary outlaw. According to legend, the two were so caught up in the spirit of the event that the teacher sang several verses of a song he had composed and cried, 'Here I come, Susan!' as he leaped into eternity. His counterpart, not to be outdone by a mere amateur, danced a lively jig before he danced again at the end of a rope.

For a time Coloma was the seat of El Dorado County, and a story still circulates that one eager citizen copied a passenger list from a San Francisco steamer and cast one vote in each name for his home town. The population quickly disappeared as richer claims and wilder stories

Above: **The refuse of several generations of Californians, going back to Gold Rush days. No matter how mundane, or how wild life became in the old mining towns, there was hardly a one without a church such as this *(below)*, located in Coloma.**

Gold Country

California's historic 'Gold Country' is indicated by the shaded areas on the map *at left*.

As word of James Marshall's discovery of gold in the Sierra Nevada foothills spread far and wide, prospectors homed in on the gentle, picturesque California countryside. The mining was sometimes ridiculously easy, but most times it was backbreaking toil.

From Plumas County to Mariposa County, the 'Golden Chain' stretched, and even today the search for gold goes on—but with much less fervor than in those truly wild days of yore. Many of the settlements that sprung up around the old mining sites remain standing today as picturesque 'ghost towns.'

Such municipalities as Coloma and Mokelumne Hill have their inhabited—and uninhabited 'old town'—sectors, bearing testimony to the fact that nothing ever quite stays the same, and this is especially true in Gold Country.

pulled the miners away. By the spring of 1848 every riverside spot within twenty miles of Coloma had been picked over by the miners.

Other settlements developed wherever there were signs of gold. Along the south fork of the American River were Mormon Diggings, Big and Little Negro Hill, Negro Bar, Salmon Falls and many more. At Negro Bar a cluster of tents and shacks developed but another town was developing on the hill above, Granite City, which would later become Folsom. Georgetown was named after its lucky finder, George Phipps. Originally it was called Growlersburg by the prospectors because the gravel was so rich that the gold pans 'growled with nuggets.' Some miners, like Claude Chana, stopped on the way to Coloma to practice panning and found gold where they stood. Within a week, Chana's mine became the town of Auburn.

According to Hiram Pierce's often misspelled account, the area around Auburn was as busy as every other spot on the American River. As Pierce told it, he '…arrived at the diggins. The Senery is wild in the extreme. Smith and myself made a tent. The gold at this place seems diffused through All the Earth but is verry fine. Rose and got breckfast. At 11 attended preaching under a live oak by a Congregational Minister from New Bedford. Went to work. Made a small show. All of us got much less than an ounce. It is verry much like work. Potatoes $1 a piece, onions the same. At night the Wolves and Kiotas give us plenty of music. Went out prospecting & find that every foot of Ground has been turned over. It is a most wild and romantic Sene. We bake pancakes, fry pork, drink Coffey & sleep on the Ground. It is verry warm during the day. The wolves stole some meat from a neighbor's tent, taking it from within a foot or two of his head. We got 2 small loaves of bread baked at a Mormon family that had arrived overland. They charged $1 per loaf for baking & verry heavy hard bread at that. Wrote home & sent a rough drawing of the digins and one dollars worth of gold dust. My back getting lame in consequence, as I think, of getting my feet wet & sleeping on ground. Daniel Newcom has a verry sore hand caused by poison, Smith has a sort of felon on his hand caused by rubbing the cradle, & Haskins hands & feet are sore from Scurvey & sunburnt….'

Coloma and Auburn were the hub of the many boom towns that sprang up along every stream. Yet the words 'new strikes' and 'new riches' were luring the prospectors away nearly as quickly as they arrived. Gradually the gold disappeared and the miners drifted away, chasing their dreams. While Auburn survived as a transportation center along the routes to the mines and across the Sierras, Coloma faded into a sleepy little town, presently 70 percent owned by the California Gold Discovery Site Historic Park. Here stands a reproduction of Sutter's Mill, a museum and other remnants of the Gold Rush.

Placerville

The first really big mining camp after Coloma was Dry Diggings. When Indians carried the word of a new placer that yielded $96 a day per man, another stampede began. Through that summer of 1848 more and more men poured into camp and by autumn it was thriving, complete with stores, muddy streets and traffic. Here the first recorded lynching took place. Three 'foreigners' (probably Mexicans) were accused of theft and attempted murder. They had already been tried and sentenced to 35 lashes each for trying to rob a gambler, Edward Buffum. Unable to understand English and already weakened from the lashings, they could offer no defense. The miners ignored common law and sentenced them to death. Buffum himself later said: 'I mounted a stump and in the name of God, humanity, and the law protested against such a course of proceeding, but the crowd, by this time excited by frequent and deep potations of liquor from a neighboring groggery, would listen to nothing contrary to their brutal desires, and even threatened to hang me if I did not immediately desist from any further remarks.'

Thus Dry Diggings, also known as Old Dry Diggings, became 'Hangtown.' Notorious for these hangings, Hangtown was not only

Below: The cemetery at Georgetown, California, overgrown with weeds and adorned with many a quaint marker. _Opposite:_ The Civil War-era armory at Georgetown was converted to a fraternal clubhouse, but the huge armory doors were retained for their historical interest, and can be seen through the windows here.

known throughout the Mother Lode, but as far away as New York. Its name was further spread by the concoction one hungry and wealthy miner had ordered a cook to fry up. Oysters, eggs, bacon and other greasy ingredients combined to make up the Hangtown Fry. Somehow this horrible sounding dish became one of the staples of Western cuisine.

A visitor to the town noted with amazement that even the streets were being dug up in the mad search for gold. He reported that 'Here and there, in the middle of the street would be a square hole about six feet deep, in which one miner was digging while another was bailing the water out with a bucket, and a third, sitting alongside the heap of dirt which had been dug up, was washing it with a rocker.'

He also noted the street was strewn with old boots, hats, sardine boxes, empty oyster tins, bottles, worn out pots and kettles, old hambones and other rubbish.

Hangtown eventually became Placerville, after acquiring the respectability afforded by the miners' wives and children, who had come to join them. Although the town was nearly leveled by fires on several occasions, it never really became a ghost town. Many early citizens went on to make history. Mark Hopkins ran a grocery store that was begun with a single wagonload of supplies. His career eventually led him to tie in with Collis Huntington, which created the opportunity to run the Central Pacific Railroad that would link California with the rest of the United States. Another citizen, Philip Armour, walked to California from New York in 1849 and spent five years gathering the money to open a butcher shop. Selling meat to the miners led Armour to his own golden fortune. His company still exists as one of the largest meat companies in the West. Yet another 49er, John Studebaker, originally made Conestoga wagons in Indiana. Crossing the plains in one of his own products, he worked for five years forging wheelbarrows and saved enough money to go back and open the blacksmith shop that would build more wagons, and eventually, automobiles. Thus, he preserved his name for posterity in his now classic cars. These men were only three examples of those who took the opportunities offered and built their own empires.

Placerville survived where other towns withered and died because of its location on the Overland Trail. With the wagons coming in and later, after silver and gold were discovered in Nevada, the miners heading east for the Comstock, Placerville again prospered. Even into the 1980s Placerville remains on Highway 50, one of the main routes to Lake Tahoe, thriving with a population of 6700. In fact, when Horace Greeley made his famous trip west in 1859, he clattered into Placerville on a stage driven by the incomparable Hank Monk. Although the trip was long and difficult, Placerville's version of Greeley's arrival (as related by Artemus Ward, the great prankster of the 19th century) defies the imagination.

HAPPY TOM'S PLACE.
1850 WELCOME 1898
N.S.G.W.
Steam Beer

'When Greeley was put aboard Monk's stagecoach, Monk was ordered to deliver him in Placerville for a speaking engagement at seven o'clock. Off dashed the coach with such furious speed and fearful bouncing that Greeley soon decided he wasn't in such a hurry, after all.

'"Sir," he told Monk out the window, "I don't care if we don't get there at seven!"

'"I have got my orders," retorted the driver, and urged the horses to a faster pace. Finally Horace poked his head out again.

'"I don't care," he pleaded, "if we don't get there at all."

'"I've got my orders," shouted Hank, and went madly on. Then a jarring bump sent Greeley's head crashing through the roof of the coach. "Keep your seat, Horace," ordered the unruffled Hank Monk.

'Just outside of Placerville, a welcoming committee, complete with brass band, stopped the stage to take Greeley and carry him in honor to the city, but Hank whipped up the team and scattered the crowd with the cry, "I've got my orders!" '

Even Mark Twain commented on this story and how it was related with relish at least 81 or 82 times to him by drivers and passengers, Chinese and Indians, and even today any true Placerville patriot believes that Greeley came roaring into town with his head sticking out of the top of Hank Monk's stage.

Exaggeration—as exemplified by Artemus Ward, Mark Twain, Bret Harte, Dan de Quille (William Wright) and others—has long been a part of the American West. After the wild story comes the dry (and not so dry) humor of the pioneer and miner. As the Gold Rush spread beyond the original camps, the names of the new diggings reflected the humor of the discoverers. Some names were unprintable, even in today's world, while others included Gomorrah, Humbug, You Bet and Bedbug. Other towns existed long before the Gold Rush brought the prospectors crowding in, and their names were normally of Spanish origin.

Volcano

Volcano was one of the towns that originated with the prospectors. A little south of Placerville, Volcano was busy early in 1848—in fact, some claim that gold was found there even before James Marshall's discovery at Sutter's Mill. In any case, it was during the first feverish explorations, shortly after the Coloma strike, that the miners came to Volcano. Many were veterans of the Mexican War from Colonel Stevenson's regiment of New York Volunteers. Those first miners did well until the snow came, when most did the prudent thing and retired to the lowlands to sit out the winter. Yet two young ex-soldiers decided to stick out the winter months though they hadn't taken the time to build adequate shelter. They left no records but when spring came some Mexican prospectors found their bodies, and the diggings became known as Soldier's Gulch. When the 49ers arrived, they renamed Soldiers Gulch as Volcano, mistakenly believing that the valley was the crater of a long extinct volcano. The name was certainly appropriate in view of the town's later difficulties. When the miners ran Sutter and his men out of Volcano, they also triggered the 'Volcano Indian War' of the summer of 1849. One miner had claimed that the local Indians had stolen his pick. Anxious to avoid trouble, the chief immediately offered to search his own camp and if one of his men had taken the pick it would be returned by the chief himself. As the chief ran off, a former Texas Ranger, Rod Stowell, shot him in the back. The miners, to hide their 'mistake,' announced that the Indians had attacked and murdered one of their men. Rousing all the miners of Volcano, they drove the Indians out, but before this small 'war' was over there were several more fatalities. Later, when the miners found that the Stowell group had lied about the Indians, Rod Stowell and his men were also driven out of Volcano.

After Hangtown settled down, it was renamed Placerville, and taverns like Happy Tom's Place *(at left)* lent semi-respectability to getting a mug full of 'suds.' Signs of the times in Volcano: *below,* an antique car in front of the St George Hotel; and *below right,* 'chopped' motorcycles in front of the general store.

The law was disrespected in Volcano to the same extent as in any of the other boom towns. Justice was not a matter of due process, but of mob violence. Still the miners wanted the trappings if not the realities of government. When overlooked in the state elections of 1849, they held their own local elections, exactly following the procedures outlined by the local alcalde, or mayor, and newspaperman Bayard Taylor. Mistaking another Taylor on the ballot for Bayard, they voted unanimously in his favor. Bayard was reported to have stated on hearing the news, 'Had I known this fact sooner I might have been tempted to run for alcalde, at least!'

In the 1850s, the frenetic activity that characterized Volcano in 1848-49 gradually slowed to a simmer. Starved for entertainment, the town was one of the first stops for the child star, Lotta Crabtree. Trained by the then-famous Lola Montez in Grass Valley, Lotta danced and the miners threw nuggets and coins on the stage. Under the watchful eye of her mother, Mary Ann, Lotta went on to national fame while Lola herself faded into obscurity.

Beyond the inevitable volunteer fire department, Volcano boasted a number of civic groups, but the most memorable was the 'Volcano Blues.' They had a salute cannon named 'Old Abe' which figured in a little tableau when the Civil War broke out. The 'Volcano Blues,' the fire department and two other organizations banded together to become the Union Volunteers. The cannon was wheeled out when a group of Confederate sympathizers threatened to corner the gold for Confederate uses. If someone had thought to provide cannonballs, 'Old Abe' might have been a more effective threat, but some round stones seemed to have discouraged the Southern element from any other action than talk.

One of Volcano's biggest problems was the constant presence of highway bandits. The bandits were apparently informed by insiders at the local shipping companies as to shipment schedules and ladings, and both Wells Fargo and Adams Express eventually had to close their offices because of this. The miners' suspicions of the presence of 'insiders' were probably true, as they shipped a few crates of rocks as decoys and the bandits had left them alone—and when gold was shipped the bandits invariably pounced.

Although Wells Fargo closed because of the many robberies, the building itself has survived into the present along with the original jail and the old St George Hotel which is still in operation. Off of Highway 49, the little town of Volcano today is one of the highlights of any tour of the Mother Lode country.

Fiddletown

Christened by the Missourians who founded it, Fiddletown had the right name for a place at which the long wet winters allowed miners to do nothing but sit around and play all the old favorite tunes from back home on their violins. The camp was just as 'wide-open' as any other. Comfortable in its am-

Below: **Fiddletown brickwork.** ***Below right:*** **This ghostly old house in Fiddletown has fireproof iron doors: in Gold Rush days, many towns lacked fire departments.** ***Above right, both:*** **Eerie views of Fiddletown's cemetery.** ***Below left:*** **A historic marker.**

biguous geographic location between El Dorado and Calaveras counties, Fiddletown was happy to vote with El Dorado—but when tax time came, it stood squarely in the middle. Even Fiddletown's two judges acknowledged its lawlessness. On one occasion Judge Yates listened through a long aimless story 'explaining' an incident. He lost patience as the outlandish story finally ended. Banging his gavel he announced, 'This court is adjourned!' Allowing the moment to extend into silence he then roared, 'This man is a damned liar!' Having made this statement during adjournment, he promptly gavelled court back into session.

Fiddletown had problems similar to those of Volcano. Once, 9000 dollars was taken from the Wells Fargo office. Five men were arrested on the 'solid' basis of their bad reputations. Since the good citizens of Fiddletown had no evidence, it was decided that the three should be taken out to be hoisted by the neck until they confessed to the crime. It seemed like a good idea at the time but, although there was much effort expended, there were no confessions and once the sheriff arrived from Jackson, no prisoners.

Bret Harte's story, 'An Incident In Fiddletown,' still evokes the atmosphere of those mad days of the Gold Rush in Fiddletown. Today's Fiddletown is a picturesque little village in the Sierra foothills, having preserved a number of the original buildings—including a 'rammed earth' adobe structure built by the Chinese 49ers.

Many Chinese immigrants made good during the Gold Rush—both as miners and as merchants. *Below:* The Chew Kee Store in Fiddletown. *At right:* A plaque which stands to the right of same (see the text; above). *Opposite:* This structure stands across the road from Fiddletown's haunted-looking cemetery (see page 43).

PLYMOUTH

These pages: Main Street, in Plymouth, California, circa 1925. Like many Gold Country towns and villages, Plymouth began as a miner's town. Families then took root, and the place 'got civilized.' Plymouth's gold workings continued long past the Gold Rush, and while newfangled 'horseless carriages' add a modern note to the scene on these pages, one's impression is still of the Old West.

I.O.O.F.
I.O.O.F. BLDG.
HISTORICAL LANDMARK NO. 256

Mokelumne Hill

Also founded in the first days of the Gold Rush in 1848 was Mokelumne Hill. Within a year 'Mok Hill' was a thriving canvas tent camp. At first, the miners were on the verge of starvation, because no one wanted to take the time to go for more supplies. Finally a man named Syrec went to Stockton, returning with food, supplies and a tent with which he set up a store. Other businesses in tents mushroomed on the hill. Later buildings were more sturdy, but in 1854 a fire leveled the camp and the more practical shopkeepers then rebuilt with stone.

Mokelumne Hill was just as violent as Fiddletown and probably more famous, not only because of its ongoing feud with neighboring Jackson, but also because of the 'Chilean War.' In December of 1849 the other miners ran a group of Chileans—Doctor Concha and his miners—off their claims in 'Chile' Gulch. Concha and some other mine owners had taken claims in the names of their miners, thereby enriching themselves—since those placers were so rich that they were parceled out in 16 square foot lots, one to a man. Bitterly resenting this unfair practice, the other miners passed strict laws limiting the Chileans' claims, then tried to banish them from the workings. After being evicted, Doctor Concha went to Stockton and got a warrant for the arrest of the 'Americans.' In retaking his claims, two Americans were killed and 13 prisoners were captured by the Chileans. A posse was then rushed into Mokelumne Hill from Stockton. But that same night, before the posse arrived, the prisoners managed to free themselves and capture the Chileans. After a hurried 'trial' in Mokelumne Hill, three Chileans were hung and a number of others received lesser punishments. The repercussions of this reached all the way to South America.

Below: The main street in Mokelumne Hill, early in this century. Evident in its dilapitated buildings is the town's 'big slowdown' after the mining days. Now, 'Mok Hill' is a thriving village with many a historic building *(opposite)* carefully preserved. *Above:* The Butte Store, on Highway 49, near Mokelumne Hill.

SALOON

Not all Gold Rush towns folded up and died. As is evidenced by Mokelumne Hill's historic Hotel Legere *(at left)*, some towns just apply a new coat of paint, find a new means of making a living, and keep on! These days, Mokelumne Hill's future seems alive and assured, as is indicated by this lively soap box derby *(above)*.

Undeterred by the publicity from the 'Chilean War,' the miners at Mokelumne Hill later attempted to jump the claims of some Frenchmen. The French dug in for a fight but made the fatal error of proudly planting the Tricolor banner. This action roused the American miners who gathered together, drove the French off their claims and carried off a fortune in high-grade ore. This piracy was not only condoned in Mokelumne Hill but was later dignified by calling it the 'French War.'

The Chinese also had their space at 'Mok Hill.' At one point, about 2000 Chinese lived and worked in the town. But fire, the scourge of every camp, wiped out their shacks, washhouses, the Joss house (temple) and most of the adobe building where they sold Chinese slave girls at auction.

Many non-Americans and other minorities were treated as badly as the Chileans and the French, and one story from Mokelumne Hill tells of a young American black man who asked the miners where was a good place to dig. The miners thought it a priceless joke to direct him to a hill that had been combed over and picked dry. Not knowing there wasn't supposed to be gold there, he hit pay dirt and was seen in town about a week later with a poke of gold dust. His new-found 'friends' then rushed the hill and appropriated his claims. This was a common occurrence throughout the gold country. A man's color was not too important when he had gold to pay his way. Almost anyone would eat, drink and gamble with him, at least until his gold was gone.

Yet in the gold country a man's background was the most private thing about him. Nicknames abounded. Sailor Jack, Dutch Jake, Three-Fingered Jack, Red Rover, Rattlesnake Dick and Pious Pete were only a few examples of the many nicknames. It wasn't too healthy to inquire too deeply into a man's past unless he volunteered it. A popular saying in the gold fields was:

> Oh, what was your name in the States?
> Was it Thompson, or Johnson or Bates?
> Did you flee for your life,
> Or murder your wife?
> Say, what was your name in the States?

Eventually Mokelumne Hill did become 'refined.' There was even a theater, complete with a stage and candle footlights. One eager young actor played the lead in Richard III. The miners took his role much less seriously than he did. The play was going well until he rushed forward, sank to his knees and shouted, 'My kingdom for a horse!' A burro the miners had smuggled under the stage began braying loudly, probably prompted by the smugglers themselves. In the confusion, one of the stagehands raised the footlights, catching Richard in the nose with a candle. The house roared with laughter as the outraged actor fled the scene, his talents lost forever to Mokelumne Hill.

Jackson

Between the antics of Mokelumne Hill and its rival, nearby Jackson, Calaveras County was kept busy. Both towns were equally lawless. Mokelumne Hill had at least two lynchings and once reported five killings in one week. Jackson was supposed to have hung 10 to 15 men from the same execution tree (according to who was telling the story). Jackson was originally a way station on the road from Sacramento to Mokelumne Hill. Before the gold was found, Jackson was a stopover for teamsters called Bottileas (which is Spanish for bottles) because it was identifiable by the empty bottles the teamsters tossed aside. When gold was discovered, a mining camp flourished on the site, and by 1850, its name was changed to Jackson, a town that was soon destined to become a center for quartz mining. Quartz mining was much more difficult than simply panning or rocking the gold out. The miners dug trenches or short tunnels along the vein of gold bearing quartz. It was normally believed that deep shafts were simply too expensive to dig and operate. Yet, here were the Kennedy and Argonaut mines, both of which proved that deep shaft mining could be profitable. Unfortunately, the Argonaut Mine was also the scene of one of the greatest mining tragedies in California history. Fire broke out in the depths of the mine and 47 miners were trapped below. They died from poisonous gases, and one miner left a last message on the mine's wall, 'Gas too strong 3am.'

One of the most famous miners in Jackson was Madame Pantaloons, who shocked the other miners by wearing men's work clothes, something that was simply not done in those days. Rejecting all offers of help, she pulled about one hundred thousand dollars worth of gold out of her mine before she sold it.

Calaveras County was formed in 1850 and the county seat was won by Double Springs. Because Double Springs only had one building, both Jackson and Mokelumne Hill considered its selection as a personal insult. In July 1851, they compelled an election to be held to determine a new county seat. As Mokelumne Hill had a larger population, it naturally won—at least according to Colonel Collyer, the county clerk. Not willing to concede the election quite so quickly, three citizens of Jackson rode to Double Springs and invited all in the county courthouse to join in a round of drinks saluting Mokelumne Hill. Even Collyer complied, and since the courthouse was also the saloon they were able to waste no time in setting up the drinks. While the toast was in progress, one Jackson man snatched up the official records and ballots, threw them into a wagon and rushed to Jackson. By the time Col-

***At right:* A visitor exits from Jackson, California's historic National Hotel, which is adorned with a bouquet of flags for America's Bicentennial celebration in 1976. *Below:* Once the main enterprises of Jackson, the Kennedy Mine (foreground) and the Argonaut Mine (background) were gold quartz shaft mines.**

lyer arrived, Judge Smith had already recounted the ballots and declared Jackson the new county seat.

Although Colonel Collyer accepted the situation and set up his office in Jackson, when the next election day arrived, he simply locked all the ballots into his desk. Judge Smith then broke into the desk and counted the ballots, finding that Collyer had lost his position as county clerk. Unfortunately, Collyer threatened to shoot Judge Smith on sight and lost again, this time to a bullet from Judge Smith's revolver.

Actually, Jackson only lasted nine months as the county seat. Mokelumne Hill regained the seat in the next election, so Jackson and its neighboring camps declared themselves to be a new county, Amador County, and Jackson was again a county seat. Such was county government in the Gold Rush days. The town with the fastest buckboard often won the election.

Jackson also boasted the last surviving bordello in California. The brothel was not only ignored, but condoned, by Jackson's citizens and any sheriff attempting to close it was immediately fired. Finally, however, the law did prevail and it was closed in 1956. The population commemorated the occasion by putting up a plaque which read 'World's oldest profession flourished fifty yards east of this plaque for many years until this most perfect example of free enterprise was padlocked by unsympathetic politicians.' The first plaque was reported to have been stolen immediately.

Such was the life of Jackson, Mokelumne Hill, Chile Gulch, Double Springs and the innumerable other camps that filled the area. Most faded away with the years, leaving a few buildings and many memories. Only Mokelumne Hill—which is now part ghost town—and Jackson survived.

Above: The last message of the Argonaut Mine disaster victims (see page 52). _Below:_ A view of present-day Jackson, with mining equipment in evidence. _At right:_ The old antique store in downtown Jackson, complete with weathered facade, and busted-down wagon. Jackson was, at times, a county seat (see text, this page).

ANTIQUES

San Andreas

In 1866 Mokelumne Hill finally turned over the seat of county government to San Andreas, where it remains to this day. Begun in 1848 by Mexican miners, San Andreas was one of the first camps to suffer from the violence that characterized all the gold camps. The American miners were not interested in any of the Mexican towns until gold was discovered. They then overran the Latinos, jumping claims and driving the Mexican settlers out. One miner, however, struck back. Here in San Andreas, at least according to legend, began the infamous career of the great 'bandito' Joaquin Murieta. Although the legend does not specify how long Joaquin's rampage lasted, it does leave the impression that Murieta haunted the Mother Lode for many years. In reality, the newspapers of the day reported a 'Joaquin' who terrorized Amador, Calaveras, and Mariposa Counties for only two months, from January to early March 1853.

The first recorded appearance of Joaquin Murieta was the incident of 23 January 1853. Suspected of horse theft, he was captured by a pair of Americans near San Andreas, but quickly rescued from his two captors by three other Mexicans. Reinforced by three additional men, the Americans chased the bandits to Calaveritos Creek. There the five found that the group of Mexicans had grown to 12. Chased in a running gun battle, the Americans escaped to San Andreas, while the Mexicans then went on to 'Yackee Camp,' shooting at every miner they saw. After killing one man, they went to a nearby quartz mill and murdered two more before going into hiding.

Below: **The countenance of Joaquin Murieta, the famous bandit of the Motherload camps.** ***At right:*** **The main street of San Andreas, California, which figured in the adventures of Murieta, his gang, and their pursuers (see text, this page).**

CALAVERAS COUNTY LIBRARY
REAL ESTATE

DUFF CHAPMAN
STOCK BROKER
CURILICH LN.

The whole Calaveras community was outraged by these acts. Mass meetings were held and resolutions were passed, ordering the entire Mexican population (not already run off their claims in earlier incidents) to leave the county. Three Mexicans were taken and hung under the assumption that they were part of Murieta's gang. For the next two weeks Murieta and his band hid from the roaming posses, but by February one of the gang, alleged to be Joaquin's brother, was captured and hung at Angel's Camp. Murieta's gang headed north and forced the ferryman at Winter's Bar to take them across the Mokelumne River.

On 8 February, the gang attacked the Chinese camp near Big Bar on the Cosumnes River, massacring six people and carrying away $6000. On 12 February, three of the gang were surprised by a posse and escaped with only one horse—two of the men rode as the other ran, holding the horse's tail. The horse was then shot but the men escaped into the brush. Doubling northward, they killed three Chinese and one American near Jackson.

Northern Calaveras County (now part of Amador County) rose up in fury. One man was captured on the Mokelumne River and hung at Jackson by the mob. The frenzy escalated as Murieta's gang robbed a German traveler and a 20-man posse rode out of Jackson, running into four of the outlaws, including Murieta. In the ensuing battle, one outlaw was killed and Murieta himself was wounded in the cheek. Nevertheless, the outlaws escaped.

Within two weeks Murieta and his gang made themselves the terror of the mines in the southern part of Calaveras County. Settlers were

***At left:* This back street of San Andreas shows many an old and worn facade on buildings that date back to the Gold Rush. *Below:* California's Highway 49 links the 'Golden Chain' of Gold Rush Towns from way up north to way down south. Note the locations of San Andreas, Coloma and other historic towns mentioned in the text.**

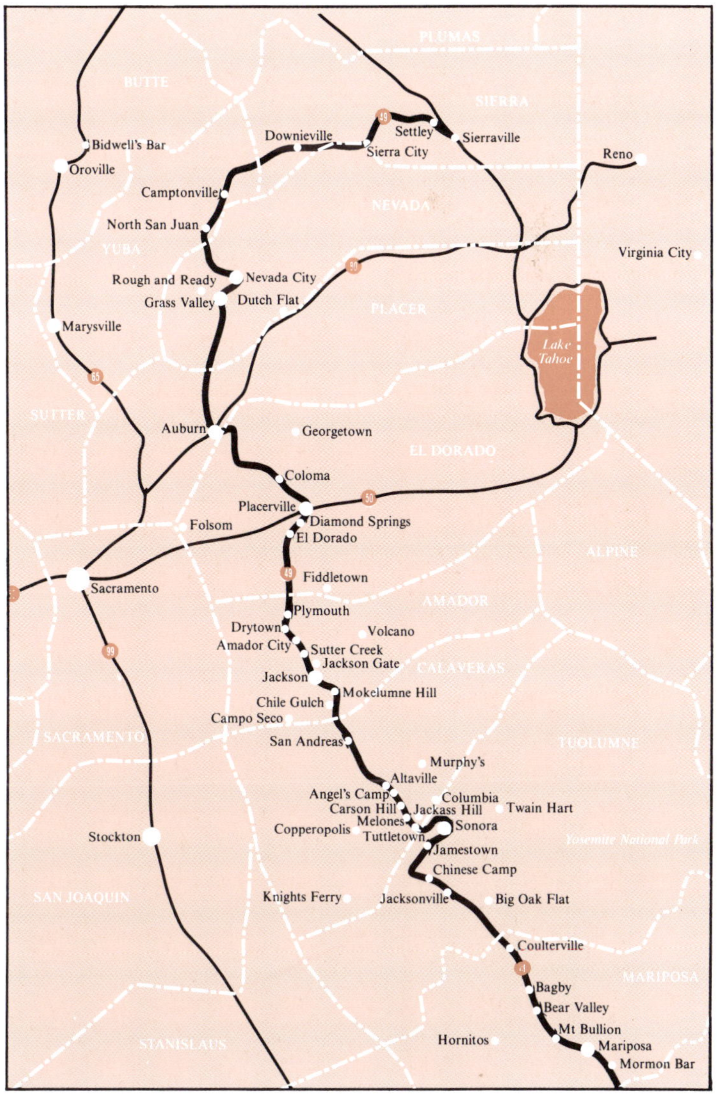

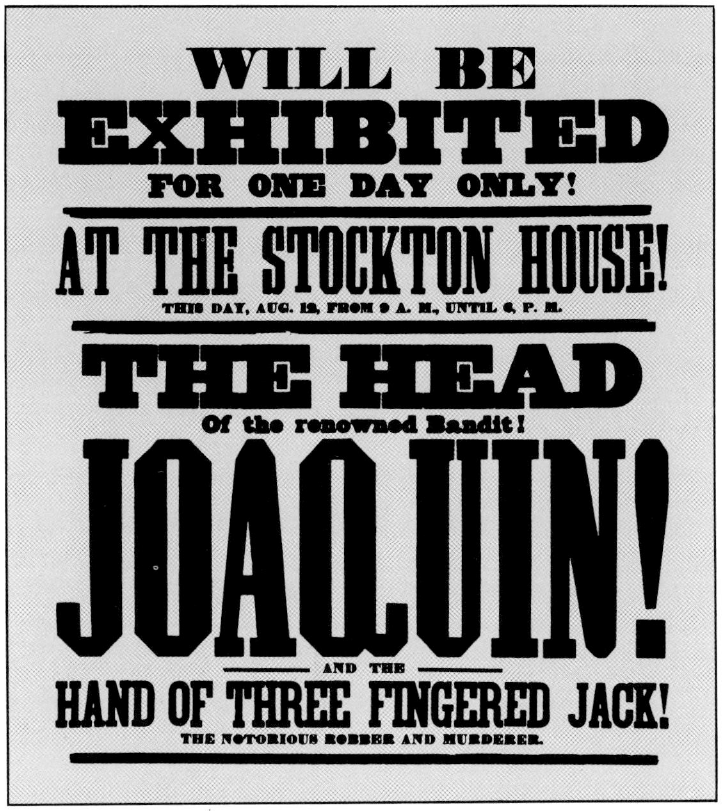

Above: Notice of an exhibition of Joaquin Murieta's head (see text, this page). *Below:* Death came to young and old in the Gold Rush. *Above opposite:* An outbuilding of Angel's Mine at Angels Camp, California. *Below opposite:* A view of the historic 'Angels Beer Hall' at Angels Camp. *Overleaf:* Mining history at Angels Camp.

panicked, at least two posses were out, there was a $1000 reward offered and the Chinese were leaving their isolated camps and gathering together in large settlements for protection. The *Calaveras Chronicle* reported: 'It is to be regretted that, so insecure is life now considered in this county, in consequence of the recent outrages, that there is a perceptible falling off in the population.'

After his last daring escape from the infuriated posses, Murieta apparently left Calaveras County forever. He was next reported about 75 miles south of San Andreas in Hornitos—in Mariposa County—playing cards and drinking freely in a saloon until his men dragged him away. Finally, on 25 May, Captain Harry Love and his Rangers came upon a gang of Mexicans north of what is now Coalinga in the San Joaquin Valley. During the fight they killed the leader of this band along with Manuel 'Three-Fingered Jack' Garcia, another well-known cutthroat. To prove the leader of this gang had actually been the legendary Joaquin Murieta, they brought back his head along with Three-Fingered Jack's hand in a keg of brandy. It was obvious that the hand had belonged to 'Three-Fingered Jack' but, although affidavits were gathered, as soon as the head was put on display, many witnesses denied that it really was Joaquin. Whether Murieta was really killed or went into permanent hiding will never be known. The head was lost sometime around the time of the San Francisco Earthquake of 1906.

Another bandit of San Andreas fame was Black Bart. Robbing his first stage in 1875, he was soon well known by his shotgun, stern voice, careful research and calm demeanor. Over the next eight years he stopped 28 stages. He left no clues except in two early robberies when he left a bit of poetry signed by 'Black Bart, the P08' (PO-eight, a pun for poet):

> I've labored long and hard for bread,
> for honor and for riches.
> But on my corns too long you've tread,
> you fine-haired sons of Bitches!

Finally, on 3 November 1883, Black Bart stumbled. As the stagecoach from Sonora rolled westward toward Copperopolis, the lone passenger, a boy, wanted to do some hunting, so the driver agreed to pick him up on the other side of a large hill. A few minutes later, around a bend in the road, Black Bart stopped the stage with his shotgun. However, he found problems immediately. The Wells Fargo chest was bolted to the floor of the coach. Bart ordered the driver to take the horses on over the hill while he opened the chest. On the other side of the hill, however, was the young hunter and he gave his rifle to the driver, who had been disarmed by Black Bart. The driver came back over the hill just as Bart was leaving with the loot and, firing three shots, hit the legendary bandit. During his desperate escape, Bart left his handkerchief which had an identifying laundry mark. Wells Fargo detectives traced it to a dapper little man in San Francisco named Charles Bolton, who had been leading a double life for eight years. Taken back to San Andreas, Black Bart's trial was the biggest sensation in that part of the Gold Country since the beginning of the Gold Rush. Bart pleaded guilty, cutting the trial short but made a long speech to make up for it. He was sentenced and served a few years in San Quentin, fading from history after his release. Perhaps this was a light punishment, but Bart had never fired his shotgun and had always been polite while robbing the stages. In fact, it was reported that once he even returned the hand bag of an overexcited lady.

Although San Andreas remains a viable town in Northern California, the history of the town remains an integral part of the Gold Rush. Its Main Street is still the same Mexican style thoroughfare: narrow with high sidewalks. The old courthouse is now a museum and the former jail out in back still stands. The buildings have been restored but the old cemetery echoes the ghostly aura of the old days, with its many worn markers and unmarked graves.

Angels Camp

Near San Andreas lies Angels Camp. Founded by a man with the improbable name of Bennager Rasberry, Angels Camp was originally a worked-out placer claim surrounded by rocky hills and jackrabbits. If it weren't for the rabbits it is possible that gold in that locale might never have been discovered. Rasberry was out shooting rabbits one day when the ramrod jammed in his rifle's barrel. Curses and muscles didn't work. Losing his temper entirely, Rasberry angrily fired the rifle at a rock a few feet away. The ramrod shattered against and scuffed the rock, revealing a gleam of gold. It seems safe to assume that Rasberry quickly forgot all about the rabbits. After he filed his claim, he became the richest man in the camp that eventually grew up around him.

One of the first men to arrive in Rasberry's camp was George Angel. Playing it safe, he set up a trading post before looking for gold. He did well enough in his digs—a few ounces a day—but it was his trading post that gave the growing town its name: Angels Camp.

Like all the mining camps, Angels Camp was eager for the *formalities* of the law but not too enthusiastic about the application of due process. For example, one miner had killed another simply for calling him a 'hog thief,' and although the charge was true, the slur itself would not have been considered a capital offense in most jurisdictions. Some of the miners felt that the defamed pig pilferer should be strung up immediately. The county authorities in San Andreas heard a rumor of a

LIGHTNER MINE
THIS MINE SITE WAS LOCATED IN 1855 BY PETER CAMERON. A.M. WOOD, WILLIAM POWELL AND C.G. LAKE. LIGHTNER MINING COMPANY ORGANIZED AND OPERATED FROM 1896-1915 A 40 STAMP MILL CRUSHED 500,000 TONS OF ORE FROM VEIN WHICH WIDENED TO 120'. ORE STOPPED AT 700' AND CAVE-IN OCCURRED. A NEW 900' SHAFT FAILED TO LOCATE VEIN. TOTAL PRODUCTION FROM THE MINE WAS $6,000,000.

Above: **This old photograph was taken at a time when much of Angels Camp had become a ghost town. The town is now alive and kicking (see text column at right), but the water wheel is gone. Such tale-tellers as Mark Twain (who is shown *opposite* with his California cabin) and Bret Harte immortalized Angels Camp.**

lynching and sent out the sheriff and a posse. When the packed courtroom heard that the sheriff was coming, the miners 'hurried' the trial, seizing the court officials and hustling the prisoner to the hanging tree. By the time the sheriff arrived the prisoner was dangling and the crowd had dispersed, probably to the nearest saloon.

Angels Camp was a center of California folklore, enriched by some of the tales of Joaquin Murieta and the robberies of Black Bart, as well as some of the world famous stories of Bret Harte and Mark Twain. Bret Harte spent two months in the gold country in 1855, and some of his stories, 'Mrs Scagg's Husband' and 'The Bell Ringer of Angel's' were actually set in Angels Camp. According to some sources, Harte worked for a short time as a schoolteacher somewhere in the gold country.

It was in Angel's Camp that Mark Twain heard the story of a man named Smiley and his jumping frog from bartender Ben Coons in the bar at the Angel's Hotel. The notes in Twain's diary read, 'Coleman with his jumping frog. Bet stranger $50. Stranger had no frog and C got him one. In meantime stranger filled C's frog full of buckshot so couldn't jump. The stranger won.' Twain worked these notes into the world famous story called 'The Celebrated Jumping Frog of Calaveras County.'

Angels Camp is one of the surviving boom towns of California. Quartz mining continued well into the 1890s but the town's population dropped dramatically after the gold ran out. In 1928, however, the residents revived Mark Twain's Jumping Frog story. An annual affair, today the frog jumping contest attracts thousands of eager fans. Some of the spirit of the Gold Rush remains in the rambunctious antics of Angels Camp's citizens. In fact, in the summer of 1987 a young man was 'hanging out' at the bar when another man was showing off a nugget worth $1500. On an impulse, perhaps brought on by too much drink, the young man picked up the nugget and swallowed it! After spending a few days in jail waiting for the nugget to pass through his system, he was released with the understanding that if the nugget was returned, the legal owner would not press charges. (In this case, the idea of possession being 9/10s of the law did not apply.) After a week or so the nugget was successfully recovered and returned to its rightful owner, to the amusement of newspaper readers throughout Northern California.

Mark Twain in California

The famous Samuel Clemens came to the gold country in the 1860s. At first he was busily pocket-mining with the Gillis brothers and Dick Stoker on Jackass Hill near Angels Camp. The men all lived in one cabin along with 'Tom Quartz' the cat—and Bill Gillis loved to tell long, marvelous tales, including Stoker as one of the characters, much to Stoker's amazement. Sam Clemens just absorbed these romantic stories and made a few notes when he could. Apparently no one took Sam too seriously as a writer, knowing too well of his laziness. In any case, Sam preferred to hang around at the local saloon, listening to the bartender, old Ben Coons, as he told endless jokes and stories. Gillis often stated that Sam couldn't take a good joke anyway.

In fact, it was because of Sam's laziness that the four men didn't find their fortune in the gold fields. He was supposed to carry water up to where Gillis would pan the dirt from their claim. Sam didn't like the cold, he didn't like the rain and he didn't like to climb the slippery bank. He complained with each bucketful of water that he wouldn't carry another. At last he really meant it. Sam wanted to go to Angels Camp and sit by the warm fire and listen to Coons' tales. When it became clear to the others that Sam really was serious, they posted a claim notice, leaving the last panful of dirt sitting on the ground, and they all trudged down the hill to the saloon.

The rain kept coming down, harder and harder, and the pan filled up and overflowed. The dirt rose to the top and, washed out by the rain, revealed the golden nuggets lying in the bottom of the abandoned pan. By the time the rain stopped and the men returned to Jackass Hill they found some Austrian miners hard at work. The industrious Europeans had waited until the claim option expired and then had taken $20,000 out of the claim. Gillis and Stoker blamed Sam for their loss.

'If it hadn't been for wanting to hear more yarns, he might have carried on.'

'And if he hadn't been so gol-darned, eternally lazy, he'd have done it anyhow.'

Sam's laziness left him and his friends without their fortune in gold but, because of Bill Gillis' and Ben Coons' tales in Angels Camp, posterity was blessed with tales like 'The Celebrated Jumping Frog of Calaveras County.'

Murphys

On the way to Angels Camp, two of Henry Angel's companions stopped to try their luck. Daniel and John Murphy found their pile of gold while Angel traveled on to continue looking. Perhaps the 'luck of the Irish' made them stop and their rich claim became known first as Murphys Camp, and later simply as Murphys. Not once, but several times, can the signature of Charles (or 'CE') Bolton, the real name of the mysterious Black Bart, be found in the register of the old hotel at Murphys. Black Bart never did, however, try to rob the hotel safe—although it often held thousands in gold dust and nuggets.

The old Murphys Hotel register recorded not only the visits of Black Bart, but many other historical figures. Mark Twain, Horatio Alger, Thomas Lipton, Henry Ward Beecher, the Rothchilds, General US Grant and John Jacob Astor are only a few of the signatures that grace the register's pages.

Sonora

Sonorian's Camp (later Sonora) was a village of Mexican miners that was overrun by later gold hunters. William Perkins, a Canadian who arrived in 1849 gave this impression of Sonora: 'I had never seen a more beautiful, a more romantic spot, than Sonora. On Saturdays and Sundays, the camp used to wear, night and day, an almost magic appearance. Lights shown from gaily decorated houses, all of them with their fronts open to the streets, and the streets themselves strewn with lighted tapers!'

Sonorans from Mexico had discovered gold and settled in to mine. But they were soon disturbed by a party of Philadelphians, led by a militant clergyman, Reverend James Wood, who found gold along what is now known as Wood's Creek (later known as Jamestown) at a site which became known as Wood's Crossing. Wood's Crossing developed into a roaring town, and eventually nearby Sonora became the focus of the 'lower' elements and violence soon became the way of life there. Since the average Yankee miner distrusted and disliked anyone from south of the Rio Grande River, the fate of Sonora was seemingly sealed by distrust and bitterness. Indeed, in 1849 there were more than 5000 Mexican, Chilean, Chinese and American miners all working in close proximity. As intolerance increased, it led, in 1850, to a Foreign Miners' Tax Law, which imposed a fee of $20 a month on all miners of foreign birth. Since most mines were paying well, the cost was not considerable, but the unfairness of the situation caused the Mexican miners to rebel. They refused *en masse* to pay the tax, and continued to operate their mines under the protection of armed guards.

By this time the situation was so tense that, when a party of Americans came upon several Mexicans and Indians preparing a funeral pyre for two American bodies, they immediately jumped to the conclusion that murder had been committed. The 'foreigners' were

Below: **The White House Gift Shop in Sonora, California. The charm of this historic Gold Country town is hinted at in the elegance of the house *at right.* *Overleaf:* In Jamestown, classic Old West architecture lines that municipality's main street.**

EMPORIUM

dragged into town and briefly jailed before the mob took them to the closest hanging tree. They were actually off the ground before a sheriff's posse rescued them. That same posse also rounded up all the Mexicans they could find, supposedly to avoid a mass attack if the accused were convicted.

On the first day of the trial, someone accidentally fired a gun and a riot began. Men poured out of the courthouse, firing their guns in every direction and at anything. After all the excitement, dust and smoke had settled the only damage was some hurt feelings and a few minor flesh wounds. Embarrassing as this scene must have been, the outcome of the trial was even more so. When a translator was allowed a few uninterrupted moments with the suspects, it was discovered that they had been conducting funeral services for two American bodies that they had found. Thus, these two men, and all the Mexicans who were held in corrals for the 'duration,' had to be freed. *Latino* miners, however, soon quickly made a mass exodus from Sonora as the persecution intensified and taxes were collected at gunpoint.

Eventually Sonora became a nearly deserted town. The town recovered in the twentieth century, but it never completely revived. It had definitely calmed down, though.

Below: **Both old and new buildings compose a rhythmic ascent to an old church in Sonora. From Copperopolis' colorful past: a large brick shed *(above opposite)* with fireproof doors; a former armory *(below right opposite)*; and a nineteenth century house *(below left opposite)*. *Overleaf:* An old store still stands in Chinese Camp.**

Copperopolis

Almost due west of Sonora, about a third of the way to Stockton, lies one of the later mining towns, Copperopolis. Unlike most of the other settlements in Mother Lode country, it was, as the name suggests, not a gold town. In 1858, Hiram Hughes was still searching for his 'pot of gold.' While a latecomer to the gold boom, Hughes was a stubborn man who refused to give up on his dream of instant riches. He worked his way through the Calaveras Hills, northward on the Mother Lode and into the northern mines, through the Washoe silver region and then back to Calaveras County. About ready to give up, Hughes was at Quail Hill when he spotted a greenish rust-colored ledge of rock. He almost left but then, figuring that he would never know unless he took it to the assay office, he chipped off a few chunks to take to town. He was not to regret that decision: the sample was almost one-third copper.

At about this same time Thomas McCarty discovered another lode of copper nearby. Taking as partners WK Reed, Dr Blatchy and Thomas Hardy, the Union Mine was begun. Within a few months the Keystone, Empire and Napolean mines were also established, and Copperopolis was a growing town. Its boom was in fact larger than many of the nearby gold towns.

With rumors of civil war growing, WK Reed built a toll road to haul the copper to port. Although the copper went *all* the way to Wales to be smelted, the metal provided all the Union Army's needs during the Civil War. In fact, copper was so important to the Union cause that a US Army regiment was stationed in town to prevent any possible Confederate sabotage. When the news of President Lincoln's assassination reached the gold country, the 'Union Blues' marched from the armory to the Copperopolis Congressional Church for the memorial services.

At the end of the Civil War, the price of copper fell from a wartime high of 55 cents to 19 cents a pound. Construction of the Stockton-Copperopolis Railroad was halted two-thirds completed at Milton, as the mines cut back operations or closed down. Later, through the two world wars the mines surged, then again faded.

As with the deserted gold towns, some buildings remain standing and the cemetery provides many examples of 'tombstone poetry':

> Stop traveler and cast an eye
> As you are now, so once was I.
> As I am now so you must be
> Therefore prepare to follow me!
> Prepare for death make no delay
> I in my bloom was snatched away
> When death did call me to depart
> I left my friends with aching heart.

Like many other graveyards, burial here was segregated. The Copperopolis graveyard is separated by four-foot stone walls into Masonic, Independent Order of Odd Fellows, Catholic and Protestant sections.

Chinese Camp

About 15 miles east-southeast of Copperopolis is Chinese Camp. History has not recorded how so many Chinese happened to come together at this particular site. One legend claimed that in 1849 a group of Englishmen brought in a large number of Chinese from neighboring camps to work the long gold trough. Another part of the story states that a ship's captain abandoned his vessel in San Francisco Bay and brought his entire Chinese crew to the Mother Lode. Some say that these two groups then worked toward each other, meeting and forming the town. If the story is true, the two groups must have been from the same

ARMORY

Tong, or clan. Otherwise there probably would have been an immediate battle similar to the one which involved two Tongs in 1856.

In this case, both groups were made up of miners working claims along the Stanislaus River. One claim was held by members of the Sam Yaps Tong of nearby Crimea House, while farther down the river another claim was worked by men of the Yan Wo Tong. A boulder, dislodged upriver, crashed into the lower camp, hurting no one but sparking the argument. According to custom, the only way to settle such a problem was by formal battle. Nine hundred of the Yan Wo Tong prepared to fight 1200 of the Sam Yaps Tong. American blacksmiths were called upon to make the proper weapons.

On 26 September 1856, the two Tongs met on a rocky flat near Chinese Camp. Several contraband firearms were in each force, but the weapons merely added to the noise and confusion of high-pitched yelling, gongs and firecrackers. In the heat of the battle, four American law officers arrived and stopped the fighting, arresting a small mob. Four men lay on the ground dead of stab wounds, and four others were seriously slashed.

A similar battle had taken place near Weaverville two years earlier. The preparations took a week as the American miners watched with interest. The men of the Yang Wa and Canton Tongs ordered from the blacksmith round sheet-iron helmets, shields, short swords, long spears and tridents, two-handed swords set in very long handles, huge squirt guns, and gongs and horns. On Tuesday of that week, the Yang Wa Tong paraded 110 strong, accompanied by one Yankee in military dress mounted on a horse.

The following Saturday the sheriff attempted to stop the upcoming battle, but was discouraged by his fellow Yankees. They felt that if the Chinese had made such elaborate preparations, they obviously wanted to fight. Since 2000 spectators had gathered to watch, the sheriff decided that the show might as well go on.

The battle began with many maneuvers, the Yang Wa in one group and the Canton in three divisions. The Yang Wa made a charge on the Canton center. One of the flanking divisions attempted to help but the American onlookers drew pistols and held them off in the interest of a 'fair' fight. So the Yang Wa defeated the Canton, with two of the victors and six of the vanquished dead. Also killed was a young German bystander, hit by a 'stray' bullet just after he fired into the Canton troop. Some of the people in Weaverville later said they did not expect the Chinese to go so far in their battle of honor, and a similar reaction probably followed after the battle of Chinese Camp.

Chinese Camp contained all the normal elements of the gold camps—stores, banks, stables, saloons and brothels. There were enough Americans and Mexicans to build a Catholic Church, hotel, Masonic Temple and Sons of Temperance lodge and the ever-present Wells Fargo office; several of these have survived to attract historians,

Built in another century, the old brick post office *(below)* in Chinese Camp still serves, as does this historic Chinese altar *(at right)* in Columbia. *Below opposite:* An old stucco/brick building in Hornitos bespeaks that former mining town's past.

tourists and vandals. Even an elaborate flue was built to bring water from Wood's Creek. As the years passed, the Chinese population disbursed and, after the Don Pedro Reservoir was filled, the fate of the camp was symbolized when the workings of the Eagle Shawmut Mine were covered over with water.

Hornitos

Another camp where a large population of Chinese gathered was Hornitos. Unlike most of the Mother Lode towns, Hornitos was originally a Mexican town, prior to the Gold Rush. Built around a central plaza, the main street ran along one side of the square. In the square there were dances and bull fights by night, as well as cock fights during the day. When gold was found, however, it was again the familiar story of the American miners pushing the Mexicans out.

In its prime, Hornitos was what could easily be described as a wide open town. Men walked the streets with weapons in hand. Saloons and gambling dens lined the streets. According to one visitor in 1857, he was walking past the gambling tables on the sidewalk when two players flashed knives at each other. Gun in hand, the dealer recommended that they fight elsewhere. Followed by a crowd, the two men went to a nearby lot and there began their battle. Finally, one staggered back to the gambling table covered with stab wounds and tossed down a glass of brandy. Despite his bravado, he soon joined his opponent in 'Dead Man's Gulch.'

Hornitos was also a part of the Joaquin Murieta legend. It was here that Murieta was supposed to have come after his crime spree in Calaveras County, and it was here that many stories of Joaquin and his exploits grew.

With gold fever, Hornitos grew wilder and more dangerous. One account said: 'Gamblers, girls and roughnecks...they were a tough lot, the worst in the southern mines. They reverenced nothing but money, cards and wine...blood was upon nearly every doorstep and the sand was caked in it.'

Matters were not helped by the influx of Chinese laborers. The Chinese section of Hornitos lay on the north side of the plaza. It was an amazing labyrinth made up of opium dens with ground level roofs, stores made from packing crates, a few adobes and a number of hovels. Gradually the flimsy structures were replaced by adobe buildings, the opium dens remaining underground. Here gathered not only the Chinese, but also the white miners who had discovered the pipe. The Chinese infuriated the Americans with their willingness to work for very little money. A Chinese miner named Charley was gleaning from a gulch one day when some boys came along to torment him. After a time, he lost patience and fired his gun into the air. Unfortunately the bullet ricocheted, hitting one of the boys and causing a flesh wound. When the boy ran home screaming, Charley wisely attempted to leave town. He was quickly caught, however, and thrown into jail. During the night he craved his pipe but, when he heard men outside the cell window, he decided against this form of relaxation and kept alert at the far wall of his cell. The Americans seemed friendly though, joking and laughing, saying it was all a mistake and Charley would be released in the morning. In fact, they had even brought a pipe and some tobacco for

At right: **The old Mexican clubhouse, fallen into ruin in Hornitos, one of the rootin'est, tootin'est and most wide open of the old mining towns. Also in Hornitos: the Gold Rush-era ruins of a Masonic Lodge *(below right)*; and brick walls of other historic structures *(below)*. *Overleaf:* A fallen monument in a graveyard.**

HORNITOS
NO. 98
LODGE
F&AM

SUN SUN WO CO.
For Merchandise.

At left: An erstwhile Chinese store from Coulterville's golden days. *Above:* An elevated view of the foundations—all that remains—of Bagby, California. *Below:* Another view of Bagby, showing more extensive ruins; these are part of the Bagby Recreational Area, on California's historic Highway 49, not far from Mariposa.

MINERS

him. Believing they were sincere, Charley reached through the window and they grabbed him, slipped a noose around his neck, and jerked him against the stone wall over and over again, until long after he was dead. No one was ever punished for this crime.

Time passed and in Hornitos, too, the gold eventually failed. Most of the population moved, the rumors of new gold fields luring them on. Today, Hornitos is yet another sleepy village living among the ruins of the Gold Rush. A few of the original adobe buildings are still in use, including the fandango hall, which now houses the United States Post Office.

'The Butterfly'—Mariposa

Nearly due east of Hornitos lies Mariposa. Although not now a ghost town, Mariposa was the center of a number of now-deserted mining camps. Eighteen months after gold was found in Coloma, John C Fremont bought the Alvarado land grant, commonly known as the Mariposa, or 'Butterfly.' Fremont did not want to buy this grant—he actually wanted to buy a ranch near San Jose. Fortunately, he was unable to sell the grant or get his money back, because two years later it was found that the grant contained the richest strike in California. When the gold seekers arrived, Fremont was not as concerned about the site of his Mariposa as he was about the mining claims. Mariposa was fast becoming the site of many miners' profitable claims. His ranch was huge, with 'floating' boundaries, so the prospectors simply claimed that their claims were outside of his territories.

On top of the illegal claims, claim jumping was an accepted process around the Mariposa. In March 1850, a group of Missourians went to Mariposa Flats, took claims on the creek and immediately jumped the claims of their nearest neighbors. Not being men to back off from a fight, the victimized miners raced off to the newly-elected peace officer. A huge Kentuckian, he first tried to reason with the Missourians, who simply told him off in very colorful language. By morning he was back, with 90 armed miners ready for action. The officer couldn't restrain them as they enthusiastically jumped into the holes, throwing the claim jumpers' tools across the flat and—while the Kentuckian

Below and opposite: **Big Oak Flat, where Highway 120 snakes along the route that miners followed 120 years ago when they answered the call of 'There's gold in them thar hills.'** *Above:* **John C Fremont, who bought the Mariposa—or 'Butterfly'—land grant. Due to mining claim disputes and mismanagement, he lost it all later.**

tried to calm them—telling the men to leave or see all their equipment wrecked.

In the mid-1850s Fremont had his ranch surveyed to include Mariposa, Bear Valley and most of the richest claims. The miners who had worked those areas for years were outraged. In 1857, the Merced Mining Company jumped the Black Drift and Josephine mines, which were now Fremont's claims. Fremont chose to file a lawsuit instead of resorting to violence and, while his lawyers were sucking him dry, the claim jumpers were eyeing his last mine, the Pine Tree.

Fremont's family arrived in the summer of 1858. His young wife, Jesse, her three children and several companions made a happy group. For Jesse, a child of eastern society, the freedom of the ranch was a wonderful adventure. Unfortunately, her serenity was shattered in just a few weeks when on 9 July, more than 50 men went to jump the Pine Tree Mine. Fremont's words to his men, upon hearing of the attack, were, 'They'll find they have jumped the wrong man.'

Fremont was one step ahead of the attackers, having already stationed six well-armed men inside the mine. The Merced Mining Company men were unable to enter. The defenders, who had the advantage of position, had rolled barrels of gun powder into the mine and swore they'd blow it up before surrendering. In the face of such determined resistance, the Merced men settled in for a siege. They posted men at the Black Drift Mine, which connected with the Pine Tree, and along the trails.

Quickly Fremont lay siege to the besiegers. The sheriff arrived and ordered the Merced men to leave. Openly ignored, he left, returning with warrants. Only four men surrendered.

Fremont had already given up on any local assistance and was trying to send men to Sacramento to ask for the state militia. But the Merced

Below: **Gold Rush construction methods are open for examination at this ruin at Bear Valley. A familiar Gold Country configuration is this metal-doored 'keep'** *(above). At right:* **Highway 49 at Bear Valley, near county route J16—which takes you to Hornitos.** *Below right:* **Oso (Spanish for 'Bear') Hall museum at Bear Valley.**

MERCED
J16
COUNTY
HORNITOS 11
30

Chevron
SIMPSON & TRABUCCO
OSO HALL
GROCERIES

men were guarding the passes and intercepted each messenger. One of Jesse Fremont's friends, a man named Douglas, decided to try to get to Sacramento. The young Englishman somehow evaded the guards and roused help at Coulterville. From there, messengers pounded on to Stockton and Sacramento, but Fremont had no way of knowing that help was on the way.

The Merced group sent a letter to the ranch, offering to withdraw if Fremont agreed to leave the mine in the charge of a neutral group until the lawsuit was settled. Fremont refused. Their next plan was to attack the men inside the Pine Tree by coming from behind through the connecting tunnels of the Black Drift Mine. Luckily this plan was overheard. One of Fremont's men, heavily armed, walked out of the brush and boldly approached the Pine Tree entrance.

'Sandy, look out for the Black Drift!' he called to a man inside.

Having delivered his warning, he backed away from the mine to a chorus of Merced rifles cocking. They still could not fire the first shot, so he disappeared into the brush.

Desperately, they tried one last tactic. Logically, if the Merced men threatened Fremont's family, he would try to defend the ranch house and they could take the mine. A messenger was sent to the ranch with a note giving Jesse and her family 24 hours to leave before the house would be burned. Instead of telling Fremont, Jesse stalled for time. Only a few hours later a messenger from the governor arrived. The message was clear: disperse or the militia would be sent in. The Merced men withdrew with as much dignity as possible, considering the circumstances.

Jesse's peace, however, was irreparably broken. Fremont tried to recapture some of the magic of the valley for her, entertaining such men as Horace Greeley and Richard Henry Dana. Still, in 1859 Jesse left the valley—and Fremont lost the ranch in 1861 through financial mismanagement. So, although he won in the courts, he no longer controlled the Mariposa ranch, his 'Butterfly.' It was eventually divided up and sold.

Near the town of Mariposa were several camps, among them Mt Ophir, Bear Valley, Benton Mills and Pine Tree Mine. Some of the ruins of Fremont's venture remain. Nearby are also the remnants of Coulterville, La Grange, Agua Fria and Coarsegold. Two miles to the south lies another Mormon Bar, technically the southernmost camp of the Mother Lode. Founded by Mormons in 1849, little remains today. Meanwhile, the town of Mariposa, named after Fremont's ranch, remains lively, its 950 citizens carefully preserving the area's heritage.

Below **is the Masonic cemetery in Mariposa. Other cemetery shots include touching and demographically interesting monuments such as those at immediate *right* and *bottom right*. In Mariposa, a gem and mineral exhibit includes *(above right)* an old-time mining operation model, and *(far right)* various mining tools and implements.**

PRINCETON-MINE

WIFE OF
DIED
AGED

BORN GERMANY
SEPT. 3, 1822.
AMELIA WOLBERN
BORN GERMANY
APR. 26, 1831.
DIED DEC. 4, 1889.
WOLBERN

Gold Lake and Rich Bar

The Mother Lode extends from Mormon Bar north to Plumas County. Although the Feather River was extremely prolific, one of the most enduring tales of the northern mines of the Mother Lode was the story of Gold Lake.

In the winter of 1849-1850, Thomas Stoddard came into Downieville with the wild story of a lake with 'shores lined with gold.' None dared to search the mountains in winter for it, but Stoddard was sure that he could find the lake again. By May, when Stoddard led 25 men out of Downieville, the entire area was further inflamed with the ever-present gold fever and at least 1000 prospectors followed his party.

Stoddard's party, stumbling for days through the Feather River country, soon began to look at him with skepticism. Stoddard himself grew more uncertain. He thought they had taken the wrong 'divide.' Furious, one of his followers growled, 'If you've deceived us we'll blow the top of your damned head off.' Finally the miners held a meeting and agreed that if Stoddard did not locate Gold Lake within 24 hours, they would hang him from the nearest tree. Hearing this, Stoddard forgot about Gold Lake and, at the first opportunity, fled the camp. His men and the others who had followed him sheepishly returned to Downieville. No one ever saw Stoddard's face in the northern mines again. Still, the search for Gold Lake led to the discovery of gold on the North Fork of the Feather River: three disappointed German miners, returning to Downieville, found gold shining in the rocks along the river. The news of this strike quickly reached Bidwell's Bar and the prospectors turned around and again headed north. Rich Bar was a fabulous find. Nearby Smith Bar, Indian Bar and Missouri Bar were soon discovered and tent towns mushroomed overnight, making these camps the northernmost outposts of the Mother Lode.

An eyewitness account of the hazards of travel to the northern mines was given by 'Dame Shirley' Clappe. With her husband, the New England lady went to to Rich Bar in 1851. The northbound stage was so terrifying that '...It seemed to me should the horses deviate a hairbreadth from their usual track, we must be dashed into eternity...' When that section of that trail had been passed, the driver drawled, 'Well, I guess yer the first woman that ever rode over that there hill without hollerin'...'

The stage ride was bad enough, but then they had to go by mules from Bidwell's Bar to Rich Bar. Lost twice along the way, Dame Shirley and her husband finally reached the overlook above Rich Bar. From there, the last five miles were so steep that travelers usually dismounted and led their mules along the treacherous trail. In spite of many warnings, Dame Shirley rode her mule the entire way, only falling off once.

The Feather River camps were perhaps the wildest of the Mother Lode country. Appearing and disappearing almost overnight, they lived a hard, fast life. Of Bidwell's Bar, Cherokee, Forbestown, La Porte, Susanville and Oroville, only the last two have survived into the present; the others faded into ruins long ago.

Below: **A 1910 photo of the Rich Bar Store (which was also the hotel, Masonic Lodge and etcetera)—which disappeared entirely by 1915.** ***At bottom, below:*** **The last cabin in Rich Bar, circa 1921.** ***Opposite:*** **A Catholic church in Downieville, built in 1858.**

Downieville

Downieville was begun by William Downie, a Scotsman who led a party composed of an Irishman, an Indian, a Hawaiian and 10 blacks up the North Fork. They struck gold, built a cabin and settled in to wait out the winter. Inevitably, other prospectors followed and the camp grew up around the original cabin. Since the winter had intervened before the usual mad rush of miners, Downieville had a more orderly founding than most mining camps. The camp and its neighbors—Bullard's Bar, Foster's Bar and Goodyear Bar—rapidly grew into part of a vast network of camps along the North Fork of the Yuba River. The area was so thick with miners, it was rumored that news could be carried by word-of-mouth the entire 70 miles from Downieville to Marysville in only 15 minutes. The accuracy of the message, however, was not guaranteed.

Still, as always, violence was very near the surface of the mining camp. Downieville has the dubious distinction of hosting the only lynching of a woman during the California Gold Rush. On 4 July 1851 the celebration was unusually glorious, even for Independence Day. For some of the men it ended too early, and some stories say that Jack Cannon was one of those who wanted to continue celebrating, so his companions decided to go knocking on doors and waking the inhabitants to salute the holiday. He disturbed a young Mexican woman named Juanita who was not popular in Downieville. Juanita, who was hot tempered, stabbed Cannon when he called her a vile name.

Juanita tried to flee but was caught at a nearby saloon and dragged to the town square where, upon the speakers' platform still decorated with bunting and flowers from the day before, the enraged miners held their trial. Feelings against Juanita were so bitter that when Dr Cyrus D Aiken and Mr Thayer protested, they were also threatened and manhandled by the miners. A rope was brought and put around Juanita's

At right: **This young fellow is crossing the Downie River bridge, on Highway 49 at Downieville, en route to the historic 'Tin Cup Diggins' picnic area *(far right)*. Other points of interest in Downieville are the Gold Rush-era Downieville Grocery *(below opposite)*, and displays of well-preserved mining machinery *(below)*.**

neck. They took her to Jersey Bridge, which spanned the Yuba River, and strung her up on a beam. After her body was pushed off the side of the bridge, it swung in the early morning breezes until cut down at daylight. It was said that Juanita was defiant until the end but, as the in the case of most lynchings, it is doubtful whether any remorse would have brought mercy and saved her.

The entire Mother Lode was horrified by Downieville's action. To hang a woman was as close to an unforgivable sin as any camp could commit. Still, Juanita's hanging did not seem to discourage women from settling in Downieville. One middle-aged woman came to town and started a boarding house. With only a tent house, a stove, a long table and some chairs, she quickly got 30 boarders at $12 a week. One day she was raking and 'sweeping' the dirt floor when she found a large nugget. She told her boarders that night to go elsewhere as she'd already found $500 in gold. Only one month later she returned home to the East, telling everyone that her boarding house had been very successful.

On another memorable 4th of July, in 1855, Miss Sarah Pellet, a noted temperance lecturer, was scheduled to speak in Downieville. The miners, sensitive about the earlier incident with Juanita, resolved to attempt a more dignified celebration, joining the Sons of the Temperance Society by the hundreds in a lemming effect. Thousands of miners anxiously awaited Miss Pellet's speech. The saloons were virtually deserted. One of the other scheduled speakers spoke longer than some of the miners could endure. Someone shot a volley off into the air with a pistol, presumably to shut the speaker up. This led to a duel between the speaker and one of the miners, using double-barreled shotguns. The orator was killed, Miss Pellet left town and the saloons enjoyed the rest of the holiday in the usual manner.

While Downieville reaped wealth from gold, Major Downie shared a fate similar to that of James Marshall; he stumbled past more gold than he found—usually to another's benefit. Disgusted, he finally left for the Caribou gold fields in British Columbia. Within 10 years of his departure, Downieville quickly faded, the gold playing out. The church was closed for the lack of a congregation and the Chinese came to pick over the remains of the whites' claims.

Rough and Ready

Some distance southwest of Downieville was a town whose founders, veterans of the Mexican War (1846–1848), had served under 'Old Rough and Ready,' General Zachary Taylor. Since Taylor had recently become President of the United States in 1848, it was presumed to be a great honor to name a town after him. Captain Townsend, the leader of the group, built an 18 by 36 foot cabin which was for a time the courthouse, saloon and gambling 'parlor.' Here the town's trials were held while the gamblers' games went on. When 'His Honor' would call court into session he would raise his voice, telling the players, 'Call your games low boys, the court is now in session.'

The dealers would continue as the trial proceeded. Trials were often interrupted by intermissions, when even the prisoner could go to the bar and select his poison while the judge would often refer to a 'pint of law,' as opposed to a 'point of law.' The pint was usually in the judge's hip flask.

Rough and Ready turned out to be the most independent-minded town in California. The miners had made their own laws and were none too pleased when they found that California was being put under United States federal laws through territorial legislation. The men had migrated from the United States once and did not wish to pay federal taxes again. The triggering point came when a miner foolishly lost his claim to a 'dude' from Boston. The situation led to much discussion and wetting of dry throats in the saloon, all the miners agreeing that not only should the foolish miner keep his claim but they should not pay the impending taxes on their mines. One miner—EF Brundage, a leading citizen—shouted with a loud, booming voice, 'We've had enough!'

All present agreed, but what should be done? Some wanted Brundage to look into ways of avoiding the laws and report back to the camp within one week, but Brundage already had a solution ready. 'Secede!' he roared. The resolution was passed unanimously and a manifesto was drawn up: 'We, the people of Rough and Ready...deem it necessary and prudent to withdraw from the Territory of California and from the United States of America to form peacefully if we can, forcibly if we must, the Great Republic of Rough and Ready.'

Brundage was elected President of the new Republic and the miners called for another round of drinks. A constitution was drawn up and similarly approved.

The 'dude' was confronted by delegates from the newly elected government and forced to leave town. Something about their pointed

Rough and Ready, today: The Country Store *(above)* faces the highway, and the miner's house *(below)* is to the left of the store. The old school *(at top, above)* is on the opposite end of town, and the blacksmith shop *(at right)* is in mid-town. The Rough and Ready Grange Hall *(below opposite)* is within view of the highway.

guns probably influenced his decision to also turn over the proceeds from the mine before being booted back out into the Territory of California.

Then the Republic settled in to wait for the reaction from Washington DC. Would the United States attack? Vigilantes were organized and every possible contingency was discussed and prepared for, but nothing happened. Spring and then summer came and the new Republic of Rough and Ready was simply ignored.

Then an appalling thought occurred to the miners. Without being a part of the United States, they could not officially celebrate the 4th of July! That was unthinkable! No self-respecting camp could let Independence Day go by without a suitable blow-out, so something had to be done. After more meetings, discussion and libations, the miners voted Rough and Ready back into the Union. With that problem solved, the miners then began to plan the biggest bash ever held in California. However, on 28 June the whole town burned, ruining their plans of celebration. The miners did what they could, holding a parade down Main Street past the charred remains of the buildings.

Rough and Ready was rebuilt and continued to grow until about 1870, but the gold mines were gradually stripped and the town began to fall apart. Still, Rough and Ready remains the only town to successfully secede and rejoin the United States without falling into a war. Today it is yet another little town of the Sierras, just west of Highway 49.

Grass Valley

Only a few miles to the east, Nevada City and Grass Valley must have shaken their heads over the antics of Rough and Ready. Both camps were in Grass Valley, the land of mining stock. In the camp of Grass Valley particularly, the promotion of stock certificates equaled the actual effort of mining the gold.

The streams of Grass Valley were worked off and on but placer mining was not the way to get rich. James Marshall had passed through, tried his hand at Deer Creek, then moved on in disappointment. According to tradition, at least half of the camps in the West had begun when a prospector was off looking for his burro and stumbled over a fortune. Grass Valley was an exception in that it was not a burro but a cow. In October 1850 George Knight followed his wandering cow to the spot later known as Gold Hill, stubbing his toe on some quartz. As all true miners did, he looked the rock over carefully and forgot all about his cow. When news of his discovery reached the other miners in the valley, they abandoned the streams and rushed up the hillsides. After another man found a single nugget worth $500, the business of shaft mining had begun.

In the winter of 1852-1853 torrential rains had fallen, flooding the roads with impassable mud. Food prices soared. Flour and potatoes were brought in at unheard-of prices and then, as the weather worsened, became completely unavailable. Thus was born the Hunger Convention of Grass Valley, assembled at Beatty's Hotel and organized by two miners known as The Judge and Blue Coat. The Judge had supposedly studied law before becoming a derelict of the gold camps. Blue Coat was, of course, nicknamed for his faded regimental coat with brass buttons—his only outer garment. It is to be assumed that he did wear the universal long johns under the coat.

In any case, these two organized an expedition of 100 men to sack the 'overflowing hoards' of San Francisco's 'soulless food speculators.' No one seemed to have thought of the hopelessness of the task. In fact, in their eagerness to descend upon the city, no one thought of how they were to travel. Not until one of the committee said, 'How we goin' to git thar?'

No one knew the answer. Even assuming that stages were running in this miserable weather, none of the miners had stage fare. Obviously, nobody had intended to slosh through 200 miles of mud.

'Well,' said another committee member, 'I move this hyar meetin's adjourned.'

Grass Valley can't be mentioned without the account of its famous settler, Lola Montez. Born in Ireland as Eliza Gilbert, she was an exotic dancer who was married several times (not always divorcing the former spouse), beautiful, spoiled and not really very talented. Lola's scandals greatly enhanced her stage image but when she moved to Grass Valley, she spent her time gardening rather than chasing miners.

Lola loved animals and shared her house with several parrots, monkeys, dogs, a bear and at least one husband. She divorced that man for killing her bear, which had merely clawed and bitten him. It was probably the same bear that bit *her*, inspiring Alonzo Delano to pen these lines:

> When Lola came to feed her bear
>   with comfits sweet and sugar rare,
> Bruin ran out in haste to meet her,
>   Seized her hand because 'twas sweeter.

When Lola left Grass Valley her life changed for the worse, and she finally died on the East Side of New York, a pauper. However, before leaving California, Lola made an important impression on a little girl

At right: **A Grass Valley mining train, photographed circa 1900. Grass Valley was in the gold quartz shaft mining business. Shaft mining was more consistent than placer mining, and Grass Valley outlived the Gold Rush as a mining town.**

NORTH STAR

who lived with her mother a few houses away. Lotta Crabtree was Lola's constant guest and the dancer taught the little girl songs and dances.

Lotta's mother, Mary Ann, encouraged the girl and they began a tour of the mining camps. At their first stop, Rabbit Creek, the miners went wild over the black-eyed, red-haired Lotta. In Placerville, a black minstrel taught her to do a soft shoe breakdown, while from musician Jake Wallace she learned how to make a banjo ring. Only eight years old, Lotta was the darling of the Mother Lode. Miners showered her with coins and nuggets. Even as other entertainment became available, Lotta worked often—in variety shows, in regular plays and with other performers between their acts, keeping as busy as she and her mother desired.

Grass Valley was the center of at least a dozen smaller camps. Red Dog, You Bet, Quaker Hill, Sailor Flat and Gouge Eye were only a few of the camps. There were placer towns that were named even more improbably. Humbug Flats—which was at first considered a failure—Pike Valley, Grass Valley Slide, and a mine named for the notorious Lola Montez, were among the richest placers in the Grass Valley area. Hard rock mining, and not placer mining, was why Grass Valley survived the Gold Rush. Without the consistency of shaft mining, the town would have died like its many neighbors.

Nevada City

Hardly four miles away lay Nevada City. Already a thriving placer town, it went mad with quartz mining. Until ore crushers were built, every mortar and pestle from Sacramento to San Francisco was bought up by the eager miners. Shafts were sunk everywhere. In fact, some avid miners were so eager that, as the old claims were exhausted, they began to dig up the streets of Nevada City. One merchant, exasperated by the mess in front of his store, confronted a prospector: 'See here—you can't dig up a public street like this!'

Defiantly, the miner pointed out that there was no law that said he couldn't dig up the street. The merchant, angered by the miner's words, drew his pistol to emphasize his point. 'Very well, then—I'll make one. You git!'

The miner moved on to another street.

Below: **An early twentieth century photo of Nevada City.** ***At right:*** **An early photo of Nevada City's assay office, where the first silver ore from the Comstock Lode was brought; it assayed so high that a silver rush was started (see Virginia City on page 102). In the background, the old Nevada City Fire Company firehouse can be seen.** ***Overleaf:*** **Nevada City, California in 1893. It was a gold quartz mining town—in its heyday, everyone was busy crushing quartz ore to extract the gold therefrom.**

ASSAYER

The shafts were always dangerous. Often not properly shored up, they collapsed in on careless miners. One man—a superstitious Irishman named John J Kelly—lost his partner in an accident. Kelly kept on alone with his work, although he missed his partner terribly. One day he went to check the storeroom where he kept dynamite and blasting caps. There was a hole in the door through which one reached to release the latch, and Kelly was reaching in when, to his terror, a cold wet hand grabbed him. Unknown to Kelly, one of his buddies was inside the powder room and, as a bucket of cold water was kept there for emergencies, he saw the opportunity for a practical joke. Dipping his hand into the bucket, then grasping Kelly's hand, he frightened poor Kelly so badly that Kelly ran up the shaft in a panic, screaming that the ghost of his dead partner had grabbed him.

The men of Nevada City were always looking for entertainment and, in 1850, two weeks before the 4th of July, they heard of an animal fight that was being promoted. The contest was to involve a jackass and a bear and was to take place over by Grass Valley. The bear was supposed to be the most ferocious grizzly ever trapped in the Sierra and the donkey was the 'The Champion Kicker of California.' It had already killed a mountain lion in Hangtown and a bull in Sonora. Some 2000 miners showed up in Centerville for the event. (Amazing, considering that by the 1980s the town's population was only 2400!) Most carried a little something to wash the dust out of their throats and by the time they arrived, the lubrication had loosened them up enough that they were ready for anything. Each paid his two dollars and pushed into the stockade.

When the fight was ready to begin, the gate was raised to release the 'grizzly.' Actually a small brown bear, it moved out slowly, sniffing. Forced out of his box by much prodding with a pole, he ambled playfully toward the donkey. The miners waited in suspense for the rush into battle.

The donkey, however, wanted nothing to do with any bear. Rolling his eyes and laying his ears back, the donkey made two swift kicks into the bear's ribs and ended the contest. The bear bounded over the barricades and disappeared into the brush.

The victor began grazing again as the spectators roared with disappointment. A lynching could have been arranged, but the promoters had also made a quick escape with the proceeds of the event. With no other logical recourse, the miners took the donkey and started back for Nevada City. There were a number of small camps in the area, so a stop at each saloon along their rambling trek seemed appropriate. At each stop, the donkey was toasted lavishly. By the time the parade stumbled back into Nevada City, it was said that the only one walking straight was the jackass.

Thus, our journey through the Mother Lode country returns again to Coloma, the discovery point of the largest Gold Rush in the United States. From here the prospectors scattered in every direction, 'following the elephant' (an old saying) wherever it led them. From this land of dreams, they went north to the Yukon, east to the Comstock, south to the deserts, always following the rumors of gold, gold and more gold.

Above: **Dutch Flat, California, in 1855. Many of these houses were very nice by gold camp standards.** ***Below:*** **The Omaha Mine in Grass Valley. Shaft mining was dangerous, and accidents were often fatal.** ***At right:*** **In this image from 1855, an early photographer's Dutch Flats studio was captured and preserved for posterity.**

AMBROTYPES
by
O.B.SILVER.

Silver: Nevada and the Southwest

The boom towns of California were growing and fading in rapid succession as more and more immigrants poured across the western half of the continent after 1849. Men were roaming back and forth across the Sierras, searching for the riches of the mountains. Some who had come to California by the overland routes recalled traces of gold that they had passed over, scorning it for the fabulous promises of even more gold even farther west.

Virginia City

The first real discovery of gold on the eastern, or Nevada, side of the mountains was actually in 1849, in a gulch in Carson Valley. The following year, another group joined the miners there and the gulch was named Gold Canyon. Within a year, at least 100 men from Placerville were mining in Gold Canyon but the gold was heavily intermixed with silver ore. At that time gold was 20 times more valuable than silver, so the miners thought of the presence of silver as only a contamination of good ore. Still, they kept working the silver-laced veins, and explored the canyon and the surrounding areas of Washoe County.

Two brothers, Allen and Hosea Grosch, found a silver mine three years after their arrival in Washoe in 1853. They figured that even silver was worth mining if the ore was of sufficiently high concentration. Unfortunately, in 1857 Hosea cut his foot with a pick and died of blood poisoning, while at about the same time Allen was caught in a blizzard. Suffering from severe frostbite, Allen died shortly after his brother did. The secret of their mine would have died with them, had not Henry TP Comstock been watching their activities for some time. He knew that they'd found something, but he didn't know what it was or exactly where it was located. Looking for the Grosch claims was not Comstock's only pastime, as he also owned a gold mine in Gold Canyon.

Meanwhile, Peter O'Reilley and Pat McLaughlin, two Irish prospectors, tired of Gold Canyon and moved their operations over to Six Mile Canyon. They found the best sites already claimed, so they moved about 500 yards up the hillside from the others and staked their claim. There they pulled out some of the strange blue ore that the Grosch brothers had

Though there were gold mines in the area as well, silver was the name of the game in Nevada. *Above:* A firehouse and lookout station on a Virginia City hillside. Bodie, California, near the Nevada border, was a rough town which originated the phrase 'bad man from Bodie.' Yet, Bodie still contains at least one church *(at right).*

found. Not knowing what it was, they sent a sample to Placerville, California. The assay showed a rich silver content.

The same day that O'Reilley and McLaughlin found the silver ore, Comstock was out looking for a pony that had wandered away. He found his pony and rode along the slope to see what the other miners were doing. Soon Comstock came upon the two Irishmen who were running the last of the day's work through the rocker. Seeing their ore, Comstock knew that they had found the Grosch brothers' mine. Thinking quickly (and crookedly), Comstock informed them that they were on his land and were using the water from his spring. It was a lie but, on the spot, but the two men were too surprised to protest. The two Irishmen agreed to cut Comstock and his friend in for shares of the claim.

By the time the assay report came back from California, the news of the rich ore had already drawn prospectors over the mountains. In fact, the assayer himself, Melville Atwood, also came hoping to buy into the claim. With him was Judge James Walsh and George Hearst, who both owned some California mines. Walsh and Hearst quickly bought out the new mine, and Hearst also bought a half interest in another newly discovered mine, the Gould and Curry. Alvah Gould congratulated himself for swindling the Californian, but ended up running a peanut stand in Reno while Hearst became a multimillionaire.

Henry Comstock, Peter O'Reilley and Pat McLaughlin all died poor. Comstock's name endured only because the claim became known as the fabulous *Comstock Lode*.

By 1859, the new owners of the Comstock Lode were shipping silver ore over the Sierras into San Francisco. The Mother Lode had started to fade, and a long summer of drought had contributed to the miners' discouragement. When the news of the Comstock Lode arrived in the gold camps, the miners made a mass exodus, pouring like lemmings through Placerville toward the Washoe. J Ross Browne, a newspaperman, wrote: 'An almost continuous string of Washoeites stretched "like a great snake dragging its slow length along" as far as the eye could reach. In the course of this day's tramp we passed parties of every description and color: Irishmen, wheeling their blankets, provisions, and mining implements on wheel-barrows; American, French, and German foot-passengers, leading heavily-laden horses, or carrying their packs on their shoulders; Mexicans, driving long trains of pack-mules, and swearing fearfully, as usual, to keep them in order; dapper-looking gentlemen, apparently from San Francisco, mounted on fancy horses; women, in men's clothes, mounted on mules or burros; Pike County (Missouri) specimens, seated on piles of furniture and goods in great lumbering wagons; whisky-peddlers, with their bar-fixtures and whisky on muleback, stopping now and then to quench the thirst of the toiling multitude; organ-grinders, carrying their organs; drovers, riding, raving, and tearing away frantically through the brush after droves of self-willed cattle destined for the shambles—in short, every imaginable class, and every possible species of industry, was represented in this moving pageant. It was a striking and impressive spectacle to see, in full competition with youth and strength, the most pitiable specimens of age and decay—white-haired old men, gasping for breath as they dragged their palsied limbs after them in the exciting race of avarice; cripples and hunchbacks; even sick men from their beds—all stark mad for silver.'

Browne also noted the difficult realities of mining. Hard work did not always make a fortune and many men gave up the dream, returning to California amidst 'saddle-trains without riders, long lines of pack-mules laden with silver ore, scattering parties of weather-beaten and foot-sore pedestrians, bearing their hard experience in their faces, and solitary stragglers, of all ages and degrees, mounted on skeleton horses, or toiling wearily homeward on foot—some merry, some sad, some

In the heart of Silver City, Nevada, circa 1900. *At right,* these two saloons evidence classic Old West lines, complete with facades. This town grew on the wealth of Henry Comstock's 'find' (see text, pages 102–104). The miners made fortunes and lost them, and the human parade was endless across the Sierras.

UMBERTO SALOON
CIGARS

eagerly intent on further speculation, but all bearing the unmistakable impress of Washoe.'

Men began pouring into Washoe County at the rate of 150 a day and gathering in every canyon. Henry Comstock's Silver City grew rapidly and it gained a sister city when James 'Old Virginny' Fennimore had a little accident. A whisky-sodden local character, 'Old Virginny,' was stumbling through the canyon one night when he tripped and fell, smashing his precious bottle of whiskey. After a mournful moment he announced, 'I christen this ground Virginia.' The name stuck and thus was named the liveliest boom town of Nevada—Virginia City. It never did completely die out and eventually became a tourist attraction, the source of many famous stories and legends of West.

One of the most famous of these legends did not even involve a silver mine. The central character was a lady named Julia Bullette, who ran a pleasure palace in the boom town in the late 1860s or early 1870s. Julia's was the classic story of the madam with a heart of gold. She nursed the sick, gave large contributions to the Sanitary Fund (a forerunner of the Red Cross), provided coffee to firefighters and bandaged the men's wounds when Indians attacked. Although ostracized by the more 'proper' ladies of Virginia City, Julia was the most well-known woman in the area; not only a mine, but the best club car of the Virginia & Truckee Railroad was named after her. Although a lady of the evening, Julia had attained a sense of style that many of those 'proper' ladies in the upper strata of Virginia City society failed to achieve.

When Julia was found murdered in her bed, the entire male community searched for the right man to lynch. The funeral was reported to have been huge, but the guilty man had not yet been found so the impossibility of a quick lynching ruined the festivities. It wasn't until three months after the murder that a man named John Millain was arrested. The evidence against him was overwhelming: he had sold some of Julia's diamonds to a local jeweler and Julia's trunk with her furs, clothing and more jewelry were found with a friend of his. At the funeral, John Millain had been one of Julia's most avid mourners, but his professed grief did not help him at his trial. The hanging attracted even more people than Julia's funeral. According to local legend, so many men spent the night of the hanging at Julia's bordello that the

The wealth of the Virginia City claims is reflected in this elegant old French-style residence *(below)*, which was photographed in a state of disrepair in the 1940s. The wealth seemed to flow out of the mines, and Virginia City society attained a level of gentility. The mining industry in Virginia City was indeed very healthy, and operations tended to be large; *at right* is an early photograph of the Empire State Mine ore mill, at the base of Sugar Loaf Mountain.

Above: The many rumours of 'General Ulysses S Grant's' visits to almost every locale in the mining country may have been fueled by the fact that he had a son, Ulysses S Grant Jr—shown here, third from left, at the mouth of Virginia City's Bonanza Mine in 1879. *Below:* A bullion shipment at Virginia City's Union Mine in 1918. *At right:* Intricate masonry and haunting shambles of former dwellings resonate in this mid-twentieth century photo of 'old town' Virginia City.

girls were so exhausted, they closed the house for three days afterward.

Another legend concerning Julia was how she had helped to save the Union. Many of the miners of the Comstock were Southern sympathizers, while the mine owners believed in the United States as one Union. At one point, a huge shipment of silver was to be sent to New York, and Julia discovered that the whole wagon train was supposed to be hijacked and sent to the South. That day, Julia put on her finest silks and rode out with the silver train. Not one man would have dared to attack while Julia was present. Julia's sympathies lay with the North. She must have been proud, knowing that one black woman riding along with the wagons forced the Southern sympathizers to abandon their scheme to help destroy the Union.

Whether Julia's exploits were true or merely more tall tales of the Gold Rush is unimportant. Julia really existed, whereas some of the other stories of Virginia City were clearly literary inventions. Considering that Mark Twain, Bret Harte and Dan de Quille all worked at the town newspaper, *The Enterprise*, it is a wonder that even more exotic tales have not been generally disseminated throughout Western lore.

One Nevada tale that has been often repeated was written by Robert H Davis and printed in Volume 12 of the 1923 edition of *Modern Eloquence*:

'In the Pinenut mining region, State of Nevada, during the early nineties, rich gold-bearing veins were discovered in the foothills. Coincident with this discovery came the development of placer claims in the beds of the valley streams. There was a tremendous rush of prospectors from neighboring mining towns, and Pinenut became the center of much activity. Unfortunately, it proved to be a superficial bonanza and petered out in a short time. A few fanatics still lingered, hoping that a sharp pick in hopeful hands would open a new Golconda at an unexpected moment.

'One of the "hangers on" had the bad taste to die. It is the custom in new mining camps for the District Recorder to perform the services of the church and to lay to rest those who expire with or without their boots on. The ceremony is the same for both. This particular funeral took place in the dry bed of a creek. A hole six by two by three had been scooped from the gravel. The deceased reposed in a rude coffin utterly unconscious of the part he was about to play.

'"Ye brought nothing into this world and ye shall carry nothing out."

'The coffin was lowered by horny hands.

'"The Lord giveth and the Lord taketh away. Blessed be the name of the Lord. Dust to dust."

'Reaching down he gathered a handful of dirt and gravel, which sifted through his fingers and fell with a rattaplan upon the wooden box.

'"Ashes to ashes."

'But instead of either dust or ashes, the gleam of a nugget flashed back from the coffin lid. There it lay, resurrected from eternity while the late miner was being gathered to the mould.

***Below:* The damage shown here was not the result of passing years, but was caused by a Virginia City earthquake in the 1880s! Who helped Virginia City ship its treasure: *At right:* A long view of the Wells Fargo & Co building in the 1920s; and, *below right,* a closeup of the substantial entrance to the same establishment.**

Wells Fargo
& Co. Building
Virginia City, Nev.

WELLS, FARGO & CO.
Entrance
& Co.
Virginia

'Without further hesitation, the Recorder dropped his prayer book, jumped into the grave, heaved the late lamented out of the property, exclaiming a loud voice:

'"I claim everything seven hundred and fifty feet North and South and six hundred feet East and West. Everybody get off the premises."

'He pulled out two six-shooters, cleaned his estate of spectators, and put up his location notices without delay. The interment took place the following day in a vegetable garden.'

Surely that story has been repeated many times, with only the preacher's name and location of the gravesite changed. Should one search the back issues of the *Virginia City Enterprise*, it is probable that the funeral story would appear. The newspaper itself did not originate in Virginia City. It was begun in the nearby city of Genoa as the *Territorial Enterprise*. As the Washoe/Comstock boom grew, the newspaper moved to Carson City, then on to the burgeoning Virginia City where it remained, continuing to print the news, rumors and tall tales of Nevada.

Genoa

Genoa itself was another of the stops on the way to California where traces of gold were found and passed by, the eager gold hunters pressing on impatiently. The town began when Colonel John Reese was sent out by Brigham Young to build what became Mormon Station, a trading post for the weary travelers on the Humbolt trail. It became known as the last station before the trek over the Sierras, and was renamed Genoa by an Italian settler. Genoa was the first real town in what later became the state of Nevada. When the Washoe boom hit, many of the prospectors remembered those traces of gold that they had passed by and returned to Genoa. Men poured from east to west, then reversed the route as Nevada's boom became well known. The gold and then the silver rushes brought one of the most remarkable mail carriers in history to Genoa.

John A Thomson, a Norwegian, had tried gold mining in Coon Hollow and Kelsey's Diggings in California near Placerville when, disgusted by the poor results, he decided to try farming. In 1856, Thomson heard about the problems the mail service was having: when the deep winter snows clogged the passes between Placerville and Genoa, the mail could not get through. Thomson thought that he could do what no one else could do, by making a pair of skis like those he had used as a child in Norway. He practiced for a while, then appeared at the Placerville post office, stating he'd carry the winter mail to Genoa. Just like that, Thomson had a job. He carried the mail for 12 years, taking three days to cross the mountains, often carrying an 80 pound pack of mail. He took with him only a few dried sausages and crackers to eat; when he had to stop and rest, he would find a dead stump, set it on fire, and nap with his feet to the blaze—he carried no blankets for sleeping.

Besides carrying the mail, Thomson was often known to be a Good Samaritan. On one trip he found a man named James Sisson half dead in a cabin on the Nevada side of the mountains, a shade closer to Placer-

Below: The Comstock Assay Office in Virginia City in the 1930s. _At right:_ The Virginia City Enterprise newspaper office, rebuilt after a fire. _Overleaf:_ CW Nutter's Family Grocery, a landmark from the glory days of Gold Hill, Nevada.

WINES
LIQUORS
CIGARS TOBACCO

veloped in imposing clouds of dust. The whole population—men, women and children, Chinamen, and Indians—were massed in the main street, all the flags in town were at the masthead, and the blare of the band was drowned in cheers. Gridley stood up and asked who would make the first bid for the National Sanitary Flour-Sack. General W said: "The Yellow Jacket Silver-Mining Company offers a thousand dollars coin!"'

The same flour sack was also auctioned in Carson City, California, Saint Louis, and possibly as far away as New York: 'It was estimated that when the flour-sack's mission was ended it had been sold for a grand total of a hundred and fifty thousand dollars in greenbacks! This is probably the only instance on record where common family flour brought three thousand dollars a pound in the public market.'

Austin did well enough, suffering from fewer fires than most camps, but floods ravaged it, especially in 1868 and 1874. However, Austin's isolation caused many other problems. As the highest grade ore started to fade out, transportation costs began to haunt the camp: the nearest rail line was 100 miles away, but Austin received a county subsidy to build a connecting spur to the nearest depot, Battle Mountain. The town had five years to build the line, but it was four years and eight months before ground was broken on 30 August 1879. As the deadline neared, the winter's heavy snows slowed the work. Finally, with only half a mile of track left to complete, and ten minutes to finish the work, an emergency meeting of the city council extended the city limits just far enough to meet the tracks. At last the railroad had come to Austin! With cheaper transportation, the old mines were revitalized and new ones were developed. Still, the new boom only lasted a little while and, when the mines were truly exhausted, Austin began to die. The railroad itself went out of business in just 27 years.

Today, US Highway 50 runs through Austin and the cars rush on toward Lake Tahoe. Before the town completely faded, its population moved to White Pine, 120 miles away. Near there, the prospectors established both Hamilton and Treasure City. The rivalry between the

two camps went on for some time but, as another of the Wild West's most colorful newspapermen, Fred Hart reported: 'White Pine went down almost as rapidly as it came up. The mines petered and the bubble burst. Today Hamilton and Treasure City are both insignificant and nearly depopulated camps; the few who remain in them have clung on, hoping on, hoping ever, for a strike in the mines that shall bring a return of something like the good old times of the early days.'

Aurora

Like the White Pine camps, the town of Aurora, on the Nevada/California border, was another flash-in-the-pan camp. The silver was rich enough, but soon petered out. The town did last long enough to cause a curious problem. Which state did it belong to? Without a careful survey, no one knew. So, in a friendly agreement between Mono and Esmeralda Counties, Aurora was declared to be a part of California. Making such agreement was easy enough since Aurora was the county seat for both counties. Highly irregular perhaps, but it did work for a time, until Aurora was officially stated to be on the Nevada side of the border. Then the Mono County officials packed up their official papers and tax monies, and moved to Bridgeport, leaving $20,000 in bills for Esmeralda County to deal with.

Aurora was a typical mining camp, plagued by highwaymen and violence. There was even a crime boss, John Daley. His downfall was killing WR Johnson, a vegetable grower. It seems that Johnson had shot and killed one of Daley's men for stealing a horse. Daley vowed revenge. He and his men waylaid the farmer in a dark alley, knocking him down, shooting him, cutting his throat, then pouring kerosene over

Below opposite: A closer look at downtown Austin, Nevada, sometime between its glory days and the present. _At left:_ Intriguing ruins of a miner's shack at Aurora, Nevada. _Below:_ A moody portrait of Bodie, California. Bodie was _the_ wild mining town. Aldo Ray played 'the bad man from Bodie' in a 1960s film with Henry Fonda.

him and setting him on fire. It wasn't the actual killing that condemned Daley, it was the atrocities he and his men had committed in the process. Already a little sensitive about its record of 27 unpunished murders, Aurora had a violent reaction to Johnson's death. A vigilante committee quickly formed and threw Daley and three of his henchmen into jail. The trial didn't take long. All the saloons were closed for the event, the mines and ore-crushing stamp mills stopped. As the gallows were being readied, someone decided to inform the governor of the impending executions. Governor Nye wired that law and order must be preserved—without violence. The return telegram he received was straight to the point: 'All quiet and orderly. Four men to be hung in half an hour.'

Aurora was peaceful for at least a few months after this big event. Not so quiet was its neighbor across the border, the notorious Bodie.

Bodie

Bodie was located five miles inside the California border. Founded by Waterman 'Bill' Body in 1858, the town of Body was permanently christened by a sign painter's misspelling in the 1860s—becoming 'Bodie.' Unfortunately for Bill Body, he became trapped in a snowstorm a few months after his gold discovery and froze to death before he could reach his cabin.

Bodie was so well known for its wickedness and disregard for law and order that in the early 1860s *Harper's Monthly* sent a man out to 'find' a story. J Ross Browne wrote of his journey to the camp of Bodie, saying: '...The entire hill as well as the surrounding country, is destitute of vegetation, with the exception of sage-brush and bunch grass—presenting even to the eye of a traveler...a wonderfully refreshing picture of desolation...I descended several shafts...being dropped down two hundred feet into the bowels of the earth in wooden buckets...I have enjoyed pleasanter modes of locomotion...There are now

Above: **More Bodie.** ***Below:*** **A stage coach at Bodie's Grand Central Hotel, in 1880.** ***At right:*** **Trying out one of Bodie's crank winches for lowering miners in buckets into the mine shafts.** ***At lower right:*** **A miner's shack.** ***Overleaf:*** **Views of Bodie.**

some fourteen or twenty small frame and adobe houses erected for the use of the workmen; a boarding house is already established...speculation in real estate is quite the fashion...Some of the city dignitaries, duly impressed with the importance of having a view of their town appear in the illuminated pages of *Harper*, paid me the compliment to attach my name to the principal street; and thus, in future ages, I confidently expect my memory will be rescued from oblivion.'

It wasn't until 10 years after Browne's visit in the mid-1870s that real mining began, but after the Standard Mine was opened, it became clear that Bodie lay on top of a zone of ore three-quarters of a mile wide and several miles long. Shafts went down and tons of ore were hauled up and put through the stamp mills. Although the ore was not as rich as those across the Sierra in the Mother Lode, the sheer volume of it allowed the mining companies to make a high profit. When winter came however, the mines were forced to shut down. No one wanted to share the fate of William Body, the man who founded the town. One miner wrote, 'There's nothing to do but hang around the saloons, get drunk and fight, and lie out in the snow and die.'

Bodie was known as *the* most lawless camp in the West. A story still circulates that a little girl, upon hearing that she was moving to Bodie from nearby Aurora, Nevada, closed her prayers that night with, 'Good-bye, God, we're going to Bodie.' The *Bodie Free Press* naturally claimed that she had really said, 'Good, by God, we're going to Bodie!'

Bodie had two graveyards, one for 'decent respectable folks' and another for gamblers and gunmen. The second filled much more quickly. A few drinks, a little bragging, and soon two more gunmen would join the others in 'Boot Hill.' One week in 1879, six men were killed in feuds. Life was rough and short and the 'respectable' locals always had the chore of deciding which graveyard best suited the latest death. The *Sacramento Bee* of October 12, 1880 quoted the so-called 'Bad Man from Bodie' bragging of his exploits: 'Here I am again, a mile wide and all wool; I weigh a ton and when I walk the earth shakes. Give me room and I'll whip an army. I'm a blizzard from Bitter Creek. I can dive deeper and come up drier than any man in forty counties. I'm sandstorm mixed with a whirlwind...I was born in a powderhouse and raised in a gun factory. I'm bad from the bottom up and clean grit plumb through—I'm chief of Murdertown, and I'm dry. Whose treat is it? Don't all speak at once, or I'll turn loose and scatter death and destruction full bent for the next election.'

Although the 'Bad Man from Bodie' was actually a composite of the real bad men who lived in Bodie, a robbery of $30,000 in bullion really happened. Supposedly, two Mexicans waylaid the stagecoach and got away with the loot. Captured a short time later, they did not have the gold with them. One was killed during the capture while the other died in jail that night. If they really did take the gold and were not innocent bystanders seized in the heat of the moment, then the gold is still out in the desert somewhere.

Finally, like most boom towns, Bodie began to die. The gold was still there, but there was eventually more rock than ore and milling it cost more than it was worth. One by one the mines closed down. Even that Bodie mainstay, the Standard Mine, finally shut down.

There were still a few stubborn old men who stayed in Bodie. One was Mr Kane, who opened his bank every day at 10 o'clock and closed at 3 o'clock for more than 50 years. In 1930, his faith was rewarded. Some of the old mines did reopen but Bodie's second boom didn't last long. In June 1932, a fire devoured much of Bodie, including Mr Kane's bank. By 1946, the population had fallen to eight people, and a few years later the town was entirely deserted. Today, the remaining buildings have been preserved as a State Historic Park by the state of California.

Arizona

Ehrenberg, La Paz and Oatman

Similarly, the many camps of Arizona suffered the same fate as Bodie, Austin and much of the Mother Lode country. Such towns as Ehrenberg, La Paz and Oatman rose and fell with the tides of prospectors who moved back and forth across the Southwest. The heat of the Arizona deserts killed some, incapacitated many others and discouraged would-be prospectors, until a California jeweler displayed a four-pound glittering nugget in his store window. Following that, so many miners arrived on the banks of the Colorado River that William Bradshaw started a ferry and made as much money as any industrious miner.

Soon Laguna de la Paz sprang up, a center of supplies and liquid refreshment. Mineral City and Ehrenberg followed suit, but only Ehrenberg grew to any size because it was served by the river boats on the Colorado River. Light boats went downriver to Puerto Ysabel where their cargo of gold was loaded onto ocean-going ships, which continued down the Gulf of California and back up the coast to San Francisco.

Opposite: A last look at Bodie, which is now preserved as a State Historic Park. *Above:* On a hillside in Oatman, Arizona. *Below:* A newer section of Oatman, showing its Old West roots and quite a few modern influences. Oatman boasted a narrow gauge railroad with which to carry its ore to river boats on the Colorado River.

Living in Ehrenberg was rugged at best. All of its water had to be hauled in from the muddy Colorado and put into water tanks. Heat and insects took their toll on the miners. Black flies swarmed in clouds over all food, breeding in the garbage dumps at the edge of town and in the ever-present burro and cattle droppings. The town only lasted as long as the gold and the river boats. When the Southern Pacific Railroad was completed past Yuma in 1877, the river boat trade died out and so did the dusty camp. Its sister city, La Paz, had already been ruined by the raging flood waters of the Colorado; sediment filled its harbor and the town disappeared. Today, it is being excavated and restored. Just off of Interstate 10, tourists are welcome to view the ongoing work.

North lay Oatman, named for the Oatman family who unwisely camped near Gila Bend in 1851. Attacked by Apaches, the parents were killed; the son, Lorenzo, was beaten unconscious and the two daughters were kidnapped. Soldiers were sent out to search for them, but the Apaches hid the girls at a small spring about half a mile from town before taking them away. Little Mary Ann died but Olive survived and was released in 1856, her face entirely covered by tatoos that the Apaches had decided were appropriate decoration. Lorenzo had recovered, so Olive joined him at Fort Yuma. Married to John Fairchild in 1865, Olive carried the Apache tatoos to the end of her life in Texas in 1903.

Oatman grew into a sizable camp, boasting a narrow gauge railroad that ran from the mines to Fort Mojave on the Colorado River. From there ore was shipped out, and supplies were ferried in from Needles, California. But it was once again the same story. The gold disappeared and the town followed suit.

Jerome

A town that didn't completely disappear was Jerome, a copper town begun by the United Verde Copper Company. The owners were Frederick A Tritle, the territorial governor, and Eugene Jerome, a New York lawyer. Interestingly, Jerome's cousin Jenny married an English aristocrat named Churchill and became the mother of a boy named Winston, who achieved something in the way of notoriety in British politics in the 20th century. In any case, Jerome put up enough money to develop the mine, provided that the town was named after him.

The mine, called the Big Hole, produced copper, gold and silver. Jerome grew slowly, remaining small for the first few years. The price of copper fell and the mine closed. Yet this was not the end of Jerome. Senator William A Clark of Montana obtained the mine and set out to make it profitable again. He put a million dollars into it, building hundreds of shacks for his miners and a huge hotel called Montana House that could hold more than 1000 guests. Jerome exploded. In 10 years the town had 10,000 inhabitants. Jerome burned three times but the locals learned to take it in stride. One 1899 headline read: *'Jerome Burns Again! Entire Business District Of 24 Saloons And 14 Chinese Restaurants Destroyed.'*

Jerome continued to grow, and around 1910 new copper mines were opened. Prospectors and stock speculators flooded in. A giant mill and smelter were built, as was a railroad line to carry ore down from the mines. Tracks a mile long ran to the mills and over 85 miles of tunnels honeycombed the mountain. But even with all the successes of the new

Below left: Not a boom town anymore, Oatman still is favored by packs of wild burros, who come in from the desert to cool down. *Above:* A lone wall forlornly overlooks Jerome, Arizona. *At right:* A two lane winds past stuccoed residences in Jerome. *Below:* Jerome's welcome sign denotes its decreasing population.

operation, an omen of doom appeared in 1925. Some dynamite, set off within the mountain, started long-term landslides that began and did not stop. The entire town was threatened. Residents became so accustomed to ground movement that, when the city jail slipped too far down the hillside, they simply established a new street level. The jail traveled about 100 feet while other buildings slid completely down the slope or collapsed.

The mines closed during the Great Depression but Big Hole Mine was reopened during World War II to meet the military's demand for copper. Operations were again halted in the 1950s and the population of Jerome again decreased, perhaps for the last time.

Quartzsite

The town of Quartzsite itself was never a mining camp; gold had been found in nearby areas. Quartzsite began as a stage stop, built to handle traffic from the area mines, and was originally named in honor of the area's first settler, a man named Tyson who owned a water well. Thus, the stop was known as Tyson's Well. With the addition of an adobe fort and a few soldiers, it then became Fort Tyson. Eventually, a post office was added and, because of the abundance of quartz in the area, the town was renamed Quartzsite, not Quartzite as in the mineral.

Similar fates awaited most of Arizona's mining camps. As in California and Nevada, prospectors raced from one place to another, always following the golden lure which only a few ultimately found. By the time the mining camps of New Mexico had been established, the miners had scattered throughout the West.

The Arizona desert abounds with myths and legends, many of which are tied to the region's 'Wild West' heritage. One of the legends involves what locals call the 'ghost camel.'

Back in 1855, the United States government decided to open a road from the Colorado River to Fort Defiance—a region which, it was decided, would be very tough on horses or mules. Someone came up with the notion to import those 'Ships of the Desert,' camels. A fellow named Gynn Harris Heap was sent to the Middle East to purchase the camels, and in Smyrna, Turkey, he met a trainer and trader named Hadji Ali. The son of an Arab gentleman and a Greek woman, Ali already had wanderlust and was eager to move his operations to the United States. Arriving in Indianola, Texas on 10 February 1857, Hi Jolly—as he had been dubbed by the Yanks—did not find his men or his camels happy with each other. With 80 camels divided into several units, his Arab drivers complained of their long daily treks over such variegated terrain as snow-covered mountains, forests and deserts. One by one all of the drivers quit but Hi Jolly stayed on, training new drivers from US Army personnel.

When the Civil War broke out, the road project was halted and the camels were put up for sale. No one wanted them because they spit at people, were meaner than mules and panicked horses. Finally, they were set free. Many managed to survive, giving birth to such legends as the aforementioned 'ghost camel,' which some people claim to have seen in the desert, always with the carcass of its dead rider slumped down on its back. The Indians have a story which tells of a foolish camel who had defied the spirits of thunder and lightning. The camel was turned to stone and thus became Camelback Mountain near Phoenix.

Hi Jolly himself remained in Arizona. In time, he was such a good scout and guide that he often worked for the Army, assisting in subduing the Indians and capturing cattle and horse thieves. He married a white woman in 1880, but he had been a nomad for too many years, so he left her to prospect around the Quartzsite area. There he reported a rich deposit of tin in 1894 and there he died on 16 December 1902.

Below left: Once a bustling gold and mining camp, Pearce, Arizona, is now host to those who love ghost towns. *Below:* Gleeson, Arizona bakes under the same desert sun that caused many a miner to see water where it wasn't, and forestalled the Arizona mining era until some truly large nuggets were found (see text on page 125). *Above:* A Native American ghost town: The Waikoki ruins near Flagstaff. Such deserted Indian dwellings offer riches for the history buff.

Though laid to rest in an unmarked grave in the Quartzsite cemetery, Hi Jolly was commemorated again on 5 January 1936 when the Arizona Highway Department dedicated a monument to him—a pyramid with a camel at the top made of black rock, snowy quartz and petrified wood. A copper container at its base holds Hi Jolly's government contracts, the ashes of one of his camels which died at the Griffith Park Zoo in Los Angeles, and his total wealth—60 cents.

New Mexico

Shakespeare

Shakespeare (aka 'Shakespear'), New Mexico engendered many news stories that fascinated readers across the country, stories such as those about Shakespeare being home to New Mexico's vigilantes—the 'Shakespeare Guards.' Curly Bill, Johnny Ringo, Sandy King, Russian Bill, Dave Rudabaugh and other noted gunmen frequented the town and their presence produced many exciting moments.

One incident that actually quieted Shakespeare for several years began one day when 'Russian Bill' was jailed for stealing a horse. A fugitive from Russia, Lieutenant William Tattenbaum had been a member of the Imperial White Hussars before he'd wounded his superior officer. He fled to the United States, where he underwent a long slide further down the social scale. He associated with the McLowerys and the Clantons, both notorious outlaw gangs. On the day that he was tossed into Shakespeare's jail, he found that another had preceded him. Sandy King had refused to pay for a silk handkerchief and then had whipped out his six-shooter and blown off the index finger of the clerk's hand. The town newspaper, *The New Mexican*, reported the later events: 'You doubtless have heard of Russian Bill and Sandy King, two noted horse thieves and desperados. They were brought to Shakespeare a few days ago and lodged in jail. Yesterday they were loud and demonstrative against the citizens, declaring that the people of the town would have a chance to dance to their music in 24 days. During the small hours of the night the jail was visited by an armed force, the guard was overpowered and in an hour or so two pulseless bodies, stiff and cold, could be seen suspended by a cord to a girder in what was formerly the barroom of the old Shakespeare Hotel...A coroner's jury ruled that the men met death by suicide.'

A few days later *The New Mexican* had a follow-up story on the hangings: 'Shakespeare has not been annoyed by ruffians since the last necktie party. The friends of the two men who were lynched there a week or so ago have not avenged the death of their comrades as they threatened to. There is nothing that lessens the zeal of the average desperado than a conscientious vigilante committee.'

It was later recorded that an inquiry about Russian Bill arrived in Tombstone, Arizona, from the United States Consul General at the Russian capital of Saint Petersburg. The letter expressed the concern of the Countess Telfrin, Russian Bill's mother, and enclosed was a

Below: Now part of the Frank Hill Ranch in New Mexico, the ghost town of Shakespeare died when the Southern Pacific bypassed it, for its ore was of too low a grade to sustain the town by itself. Stone and brick made for coolness in the hot Arizona sun, so it made sense to build public establishments _(opposite)_ of same.

photograph. Thus, Russian Bill's true identity was relayed to the citizens of Shakespeare. Respecting a mother's love for her son, they sent back the story to her that the Lieutenant, 'long a prosperous citizen of these parts, honoured and respected by all, had recently been the victim of an accident resulting in his untimely death.'

Hangings and near-hangings kept the vigilantes—known as the Stranglers—active. Robert 'Arkansaw' Black, from Arkansas, was a bit indiscreet in his affair with a prominent citizen's wife. The vigilantes were reluctant to act but Arkansaw was finally caught. His feet had just left the ground when the saloon keeper, Rory Jay, called, 'He's too good a man to hang. Let the woman and her husband get out of town.' Arkansaw survived but perhaps he learned a little discretion after his 'necktie party.'

Indians also raided in the area, normally without fatalities. One woman, Mrs WD Griffith, always ran to her closet at the alarm. There she kept her wig. If and when she was scalped she wanted to be sure the Apache would get her 'falsie' and not her own hair.

Shakespeare is an example of a ghost town where real ghosts are said to have made a number of appearances. One ghost in particular haunts an adobe home that was used as a school in 1905 and is known for his sulfur smell. One day around 1906 at lunch time the children were digging in the basement when they found bones. Their teacher said the bones were of human origin and insisted that they be immediately reburied. Ever since, the ghost reportedly comes upstairs every few months, bringing with him the 'odor of a struck match.' Since the town has been abandoned, there have been few reports of the children's sulfurous friend. Actually, it is surprising that there are not *more* ghost stories haunting the ruins of the boom towns.

Pike's Peak or Bust!

Colorado

The prospectors followed every rumor of gold, from California to Oregon and Washington, on into Canada, back to Idaho and into Colorado. The first reports in 1858-59 of gold in Colorado attracted thousands more Easterners toward the West. Eastern businesses were still in the middle of the Panic of 1857 and men's imaginations flared at the wildly exaggerated rumors out of Colorado. Newspapers announced: '*A New Eldorado In Kansas Territory!*' When spring came the hopeful seekers set out from Kansas City, Omaha and Independence—'Pike's Peak or Bust!'

The finders of that bit of placer gold that had sparked the latest series of rumors had already moved on to Wyoming, without any spectacular success. In 1859, however, William Russell and his friends realized the rush that was coming and they decided to dive into Colorado real estate. They laid out the town of Denver, planning to sell lots to the 'fifty-niners.' Of the 100,000 who set out for Colorado, fully half turned back before ever reaching the land of gold—'busted.' Another 25,000 reached Colorado, found that the gold was just another rumor, and went home disgusted. The remainder stayed on and so were in on the *real* Colorado gold strikes.

George A Jackson and John H Gregory, experienced prospectors, did find gold at Chicago Creek and Clear Creek, west of Denver. When the news of their discoveries reached Denver, prospectors swarmed out to the strike. The new rush was pumped up by the glowing stories sent back to the East by journalists. By coincidence, one of those intrepid reporters was the famous Horace Greeley, editor of the *New York Tribune*, who was completing his tour of California and Nevada when

Below: **The three Russell brothers were prospectors from Georgia who persistently sought gold in Colorado, started the Gold Rush of '*59*, and founded the present day city of Denver, Colorado.** ***At right:*** **A turn-of-the century Pike's Peak miner poses in front of his home; it looks like he'd been working hard.**

he heard the news of the Colorado gold strike. His adventures there were told in Alice Polk Hill's *Tales of the Colorado Pioneers* published in Denver in 1884:

'When he arrived in Denver he was received with all the honor that the infant city could command. He said he didn't intend to be deceived in this matter, that seeing was believing, and he wanted to wash out some of the dirt himself. So the men put their heads together to see how they could "come it" over the old gentleman. They themselves were satisfied as to the richness of Gregory Gulch, it was no intention to deceive, but Solomon says "there is a time for all things," and they wanted a "good one" on Horace Greeley. So they sent a message to the camp that Horace was coming, and to salt a mine. The boys took down an old shotgun and fired gold dust into a hole for all it was worth.

'Bright and early the next morning a spanking team was rigged up, and the distinguished gentleman started for the gulch, accompanied by some of the most plausible, entertaining and versatile talkers of the country. They escorted him over the diggings, related all the interesting events in the history of its discovery, showed him specimens of the dirt and pure gold that had been washed out. Mr Greeley's soul was in arms, and, eager for the task, he called for a shovel and pan, rolled up his sleeves, and went down into the pit. They gave him all the necessary instructions as to the process of panning, and looked on with palpitating anxiety.

'Mr Greeley was an apt scholar, and put his dirt through like an adept in the art. It panned out big. All the bottom of the pan was covered with bright gold particles. They slapped him on the shoulders in regular Western style, and told him to try it again—which he did, with the same success. Then he gathered up his gold dust in a bag and said:

'"Gentlemen, I have worked with my own hands and seen with my own eyes, and the news of your rich discovery shall go all over the world, as far as my paper can waft it."

'Mr Greeley left, believing he had made a thorough test. As soon as he reached New York he devoted a whole side of the *Tribune* to an ecstatic description of the camp, headed with large, glaring type, such as "bill-stickers" use. The report was read all over the country, and caused a great rush to the land of promise. Those who had the fever took a relapse, and they had it bad. It was a raging epidemic, and spread faster than the cholera in Egypt.

'He shouted into the ears of the over-crowded East until the welkin rang, "Young man, go West!" It was his glowing articles and earnest advice about "going West" that caused the first great boom in Colorado. The honest old man went down to his grave ignorant of the joke that was played upon him.'

The settlement at Gregory Gulch was first called Gregory Point, then Mountain City. Another town, Black Hawk, was begun about a mile below. The miners, however, preferred to gather high in the gulch and although it was not an ideal site, in 1860 the shanties and tents became known as Central City.

Central City

Denver attracted the bankers, businessmen and other 'respectable' types, while Central City gathered an assortment of miners, gamblers, saloon keepers and ladies of the evening. The madamoiselle that ruled the hearts of the men of the gulch was the actress Mlle Haydee. She and her troupe came to play Central City in its first summer, 1859. Thus the new town already had a theater. Half the men believed themselves in love with 'Miss Millie' and so it wasn't long before a permanent theater, The Olympia, was built above the Veranda Hotel in the 1860s. Since the female population of Central City consisted of one 'straight' woman and a dozen prostitutes, it was not difficult for Miss Millie to take charge of the men. When it was heard that a gambler, Tom Evans,

had forced Miss Millie into a buggy and whipped the horses to top speed, the miners buzzed like a nest of hornets but since no one knew where Evans had gone, the posse was unable to follow. A week later the terrible truth came out that the two had been married in Denver.

The first woman in Central City, Miss Mary York, ran the first boarding house. She was extremely adept at defending her virtue but one of her guests, a young miner named Billie Cozens, finally captured her heart. After they were married Billie became the sheriff but there was no jail in Central City. It did not take long to build one, however, after Billie made the mistake of chaining two prisoners to the bedstead where Mary and their newborn son lay. Though the prisoners lay on the floor and were very polite, (they were threatened with violence if they disturbed either mother or baby), when Mary recovered her strength she made Billie's life miserable until the new jail was built.

When the boom collapsed in the 1870s, the camp suffered a severe depression. Then the mine owners came out from New York to run the mines, but made the situation worse due to their ignorance of mining. Still, the quartz-crushing stamp mills managed to keep working, and Central City survived through the 1870s and 1880s despite depression, fires and flooding in the mines.

One of the specialists in removing the water from the deep shafts was Gassy Thompson. He didn't always want to work as hard at pumping—which was a long, hard job—as the situation necessitated. On one occasion, he had a bright idea. Gassy killed a stray dog with a rock. Finding an old coat and hat near the mine, he smeared them with the dog's blood. He then tied a rock to the dog and dropped it into the flooded shaft. Finally, he went to town and spread a rumor of foul play at the mine throughout the city's saloons. It didn't take long for word of

Below left: The gold diggings at Central City in 1859. *At top, right:* Miners eating outside their home in the 1880s. *At right:* Mealtime inside a mining shack, also in the 1880s. *Below:* A view of Leadville, Colorado in the nineteenth century, featuring the Glengarry House boarding home, at 308 East Third Street.

the bloodstained clothing to reach the sheriff. Organizing a posse, he went to investigate and, finding the hat and coat, borrowed some pumps and began pumping the mine. They certainly found the body—the poor dog—and the sheriff probably had a number of unkind words about Gassy. Prudently, Gassy had already left for another county. When things had cooled down a bit he returned to collect his fee—after all, the mine had been pumped dry according to his contract.

Central City, unlike many of the California boom towns, had been filled with Union fervor during the Civil War. On 15 April 1865 when the news of President Lincoln's assassination reached the city, mourning was nearly universal. One William Tabor, a new arrival from Kentucky, was unwise enough to publicly state, 'I'm glad of it. Served him right.' Shocked citizens felt that he should be immediately lynched for this insult. Sheriff Cozens had to arrest Tabor to protect him from the mob. A telegram was sent to the military authorities in Denver. The return telegram read, 'Turn him over to the people to do with him as they please. If they do not want to deal with him send him here in irons.'

With a lynch mob threatening to break into the jail at any minute, the sheriff and the town's leading lawyer, Henry M Teller, called a meeting. The lawyer managed to persuade the crowd that a lynching would be 'a lasting disgrace on the town.' Tabor lived to receive his formal trial and the *Register* reported on 27 April, 'Tabor, the southern sympathizer, has been condemned at Denver and sentenced to carry a bag of sand weighing 60 pounds, six hours a day for 30 days.'

During the first summer in Central City, many immigrants found that all the good claims were already taken. Among those disappointed prospectors were Augusta and Horace Tabor and their baby. Horace had dragged Augusta out of her sick bed in Denver to chase the golden dream. They eventually settled in California Gulch. Hard years passed, and Augusta was compelled to take in boarders to pay the rent until Horace and his partners finally stumbled into what would become the 'Little Pittsburg' Mine. It wasn't long afterward that Horace, now a millionaire, was elected Lt Governor of Colorado.

Horace was wildly extravagant, and he and Augusta argued about his spending, his choice of residence, and especially about his girlfriend, the glamorous Elizabeth McCourt, aka 'Baby Doe.' The marriage ended and Horace married Baby Doe. Naturally, this met with disapproval among the upper crust ladies of Denver but surely Horace's money must have had its comforts for the former Miss McCourt. However, the very extravagances that led to the failure of his first marriage also led to his financial failure. All of his mines closed, went bankrupt or were sold as production dropped, and Horace died about two years later in Denver. Upon his death, Baby Doe was left des-

Below left: **Chestnut Street in Leadville, in 1878.** ***At left:*** **A miner of yesteryear, at home with his stick and his pipe.** ***Above:*** **The Georgetown, Colorado Fire Brigade!** ***Below:*** **The restored dining room of Georgetown's nineteenth century Hotel de Paris.**

titute. Her daughters were gone and there was no one left to support her, so she lived in a little cabin at the mouth of the Matchless Mine in Leadville, until she froze to death one winter.

Leadville itself never became a ghost town, but the history of Leadville is closely intertwined with that of Colorado's mining towns, since Leadville drew many miners from Central City and then lost them as they moved on to the next big strike at Cripple Creek in 1890.

Cripple Creek

The Womack family had moved to Colorado in 1861 because Sam Womack wanted to get his 17-year-old son Bob out of Kentucky before Bob was drafted for the Civil War. With a letter writing campaign, Sam then managed to persuade the rest of the family to join the two of them at Idaho Springs, Colorado. There, Sam, Bob and another son set out to learn all they could about mining. They must have learned well because they quickly found a claim with a rich vein of silver in the area in which Georgetown was later established. The Womacks, however, missed that bonanza because Sam decided that mining was too hard on his health and they should take up cattle ranching instead. They bought a ranch south of Pike's Peak, and it was the best thing they could have done.

Lacking his father's ambition, Bob Womack was suited only to a career with a bottle, but he was obsessed with the notion that somewhere nearby his family's land there was a gold mine waiting to be discovered. Everyone else in nearby Colorado Springs thought Bob was crazy, as they were sure that the geologic formations in the area were just not right. When Bob *did* find a rock that assayed $2000 per ton, no one even blinked, despite the rock as evidence. Everyone knew of Bob's drinking problem, and a prankster named 'Chicken Bill' was given credit for misleading the poor drunkard. Still, one newcomer, a

dentist named Dr Grannis, believed Bob. But because Bob's reputation always preceded him, even when the partnership found a rich vein of gold in the mine that they called 'The El Paso,' no one believed either one of them. At about that same time James Pourtales, a German count, decided to work a claim near the El Paso. When he discovered gold, he had no trouble with disbelievers, and soon the entire area was busy.

Bob Womack had managed to survive 66 years of poor health and acute alcoholism, but his fabulous discovery at Cripple Creek did not ease his last days. He died penniless in Colorado Springs on 10 August 1909.

A town sprang up randomly around the claims. Called Cripple Creek, it was characterized by tents, flimsy cabins, muddy streets and foot traffic that added to the confusion as every claim paid off. Horace Bennett and Julius Meyers already owned much of the land upon which the growing townsite was developing. They had originally intended to use it as cattle range, but with the new gold strike, they changed their minds and laid out a plan for the town on paper. They were dismayed to find that their carefully drawn map did not even begin to account for the topography. The land was so uneven that a later joke, '...I hear someone fell off Bennett Avenue last night and broke his leg...' actually had a factual basis. In fact, Cripple Creek itself was named when the first settler, a cattleman, was building a shelter over a spring. His helper accidentally fired a gun wounding another man in the foot. The noise frightened a calf which then jumped over the creek and broke its leg. These events made the rancher exclaim, 'Well, this here is sure one hell of a cripple creek!'

Bennett Avenue evolved as the first business district in Cripple Creek. Everything—from schools to bordellos—was built there, although the latter eventually moved to Meyers Avenue. With at least 70 saloons, Meyers Avenue was a bustling place and, as the miners spent their gold, the red light district spread downhill, both geographically and in price. At the top of the hill were the most expensive houses, staffed by young white women, while near the bottom were the older women and minority groups.

Also in this area were many boarding houses and dance halls on Meyers Avenue and it was in one of these establishments that the town's first big fire was started. This one was successfully put out, but only a few days later a worse fire nearly destroyed all of Cripple Creek. The nearby towns—usually bitter rivals—rushed food, blankets and tents to the many homeless. Time passed, Cripple Creek was rebuilt, and many prosperous moments were recorded in the city's history.

In 1894 and 1903, various labor disputes in Colorado led to murder, dynamiting of property and finally to the blowing up of a railway station. After this last act of sabotage, the public demanded soldiers and guards to jail the protestors and stop the violence. Within a year peace had returned, but water was now flooding many mines and others were just petering out. Tunnels were made through the walls of some mines, providing drainage so that the mining could continue. Still, the end was nearing; the gold was running out.

Victor

The founders of nearby Victor suffered similar fates. Yet in its heyday, Victor was a fitting rival to Cripple Creek's success. Although in troubled times the two towns helped each other, their normal relationship was one of back-biting and snide allusions in the local newspapers. One glowing example of such editorials came after Independence Day had fallen on a Sunday and Victor had celebrated regardless. The citizenry of Victor, stung by criticism from Cripple Creek, reported in the *Record*: 'The Goody Goody people of Cripple

At right: **Cripple Creek, Colorado in the 1890s. The somewhat varied topography evidenced here gave rise to jokes about 'falling' from street to street.** ***Overleaf:*** **At home on a rainy day, two miners play cards while a third kibitzes.**

DRUGS

Creek mean to suppress all sorts of patriotic doings on the Fourth (Sunday). Patriotism must be below par with our neighbors, for didn't they close up gambling on Friday and reopen the games on the following Sabbath? Is it more of a desecration of the Sabbath to have a drilling match than to go on a Meyers Avenue debauch? Is it worse to play baseball than faro or roulette? Oh, consistently, thy keepers are not the divines of Cripple.'

Victor was also one of the more notorious condoners of highgrading, the practice of removing as much rich ore as possible, but not to the owner's benefit. The miners developed special undergarments with reinforced pockets to carry out the gold. Obviously, the mine foremen must have overlooked the heavily padded men staggering out under their rich load at the shift's end. There was so much loose gold that many miners were tempted beyond their strength. It was such a common practice that the 'Highgraders Association' was formed. The society was soon beset with troubles, however. The miners accused the operators of keeping more than a fair share of the profits and several offices were dynamited. Of these bombings, at least one was blamed on the mine owners, who were less than enthusiastic about the highgraders' practices.

Eventually, the gold also faded from Victor's mines. Both Cripple Creek and Victor survived, remaining small but active towns. Between the two towns, one is never out of sight of the old mines. The road is the only interruption to six miles of ore dumps, hoists, shaft houses and railroad tracks.

Utah

Silver Reef

Just across Colorado's western border was a group of men with high principles. Led to Utah in 1845 by Brigham Young, the members of the Church of Latter Day Saints were basically religious exiles. Joseph Smith, the sect's founder, and his followers had been persecuted by their 'Christian' neighbors and Smith himself was killed by a mob while trying to build a place for his people in Illinois. Young, his successor, realized that the only safety for the Mormons was west, far out of the reach of their enemies. They settled beside the Great Salt Lake in Utah and, despite the harsh surroundings, began to build their own little paradise.

The Gold Rush was a constant hazard to the Mormons. Young feared that the lure of gold would corrupt his peoples' beliefs. He forbade them to search for gold, telling them, 'We cannot eat silver and gold, neither do we want to bring into our peaceful settlements a rough frontier population to violate the morals of our youth, overwhelm us by numbers and drive us again from our hard-earned homes.'

Gold was first discovered in Bingham Canyon by Mormons Sanford and Thomas Bingham but, following their leader's orders, they covered up their prospect holes. It wasn't until General Patrick E Conner's soldiers rediscovered the gold in 1863 that Utah's boom began. The Mormons couldn't stop the flood of men spreading across the territory. Mining camps sprang up here and there in the mountains and deserts.

One of the most interesting phenomena of Utah's boom was a place called Silver Reef. Several stories exist to explain how silver was discovered in a sandstone outcropping. Geologists said that silver in sandstone was impossible. The geologists were wrong.

At right: Eureka, Utah, after its glory days. 'Eureka' means 'I have found it!' The Mormons, seeing what gold fever had done in other states, quashed their own desire for the yellow metal by way of preventing a gold and silver rush in Utah. In 1863, Union soldiers found an old Mormon claim, and the Utah rush was on.

1879

One tale states that a prospector was wandering through the sandstone ridges, with the cold evening approaching. He made it to Leeds, where one of the Mormon settlers welcomed him, throwing more fuel on the fire. Warming himself, the prospector watched with disbelief as a tiny bead of silver oozed from the rocks lining the fireplace. He caught the drop and later found that his eyes hadn't deceived him—it was silver!

Another popular story relates that some miners in Pioche, Nevada believed that Murphy, the local assayer, always exaggerated his reports. At the saloon one night they were discussing Murphy's overly optimistic assays and one miner exclaimed, 'I'll bet Murphy would report silver in a grindstone!' One version says that when Murphy reported silver in the sandstone grinder the miners exploded and they gave him a choice between leaving town or doing a dance from the hanging tree. He only stayed long enough to find out where the grindstone had come from. A variation of the same story said that by the time the report reached the miners, Murphy was already long gone, having traced the stone to Leeds.

Actually, John Kemple was the first man to find the silver reef. He left for Nevada, but after much reflection upon his find and despite the geologists' disbelief, he returned with friends and started the Harrisburg Mining District.

A number of small camps sprang up in the area. One, Bonanza City, was begun by William Tecumseh Barbee, who bragged that the town was '...three weeks old and can boast an assay office, blacksmith shop, a sampling works, a boarding house...and will soon have a miners' supply store.' Barbee sent many accounts of Bonanza City to the *Salt Lake Tribune*. In one, he spoke of the disbelief of the geological experts at the Smithsonian Institution: '...but as the mines are here, what are the rock sharps going to do about it?' Apparently, a prospector had sent them a piece of petrified wood with veins of silver. And the experts' reaction to this common Bonanza City phenomena? '...interesting fake as silver in nature is not formed in petrified wood...'

Silver Reef began with one store set up at the intersection of the roads from Buckeye, White, Middle and East Reef. Essentially a gentile (what Mormons call non-Mormons) town, Silver Reef was amazingly tolerant toward Mormon values. In fact, when the Marshall was on his way to the Mormon towns of Grafton, St George or Rockville, the telegraph operator would signal the town with a coded message. In St George, since the telegraph office was in a furniture store, the signal was an order for 'two chairs.' The relations between the religious groups in Silver Reef and nearby towns were so cordial that Father Scanlon, the Catholic priest, was invited to celebrate Mass in St George's Mormon tabernacle.

Cordial relations or not, however, Silver Reef still had the usual problems of gambling, women and murder. Even St George had its experience with 'Judge Lynch.' A Michael Garbis was killed by his former employee, who was then tried and found guilty—but the mob couldn't wait for the legal execution. They took him from the jail and hung him at the edge of town. The body was left hanging as a warning, and it was later reported that the town comedian had passed by and commented, 'I have observed that tree growing there for the last 25 years. This is the first time I have ever seen it bearing fruit.'

Below: A tough-looking street in the 'toughtown' section of De Lamar, Idaho in the 1890s. Another boom town gone bust is Humphrey, Idaho _(at right)_. The Idaho miners were said to be avid, '...after any atom of gold in the vicinity.'

Through the years of the boom towns of Utah, the influx of gentile prospectors and settlers did disrupt the Mormons' way of life. One should note, however, that although the Mormons' political and economic stranglehold has loosened, today the Mormon Church remains the major influence on daily life in Utah.

Idaho

While the lands of Utah were controlled by the Mormons, those of mountainous Idaho were in the hands of the fierce Nez Perce Indians. The threat of the Indians was enough to keep most settlers out, but when Captain ED Pierce found gold in 1859, the usual rush was on. Dozens of camps were quickly established and, as the 19th century historian HH Bancroft wrote, '...the miners of Idaho were like quicksilver...after any atom of gold in the vicinity.'

Silver City

The most typical Idaho camp was Silver City. Between the Indian wars, the fighting over boundaries between claims, and the huge miners' strike in 1872 that involved five mines, it seems amazing that anyone actually had time to work. Yet work they did, the mines yielding ore as rich as $5000 a ton!

There were occasional shortages in the Idaho towns. The *Owyhee Avalanche* on 3 February 1866 reported that: 'According to an old woman's saying that "bread is the staff of life, but whiskey is life itself" we are out of "life" just now, though there is flour enough to meet present needs.'

However, there never seemed to be any shortage of humor. The Mason's Lodge spanned Jordon Creek so the Masons often came in through the front and left through the back, declaring they had 'crossed the Jordon.'

Yet another 'joke' that was not as funny to those involved as to those who heard it later concerned a certain bordello in Silver City—where some of these establishments were nicer than the townspeoples' own residences. There were always a few married men frequenting such premises, and at least one found there by his wife was added to the ghostly population above Slaughter House Gulch.

In Idaho, as in many other states, Chinese prospectors followed the white miners, establishing claims in areas that their predecessors had bypassed as unprofitable. One Chinese character in Idaho folklore was the beloved Polly Bemis of Warren. As interviewed by 'Countess Gizicka' for the July 1921 issue of *Field and Stream* magazine, it was said that 'she stands not much over four feet, neat as a pin, wrinkled as a walnut, and at 69 is full of dash and charm...Polly told me..."My folucks in Hong Kong had no grub. Dey sell me, slave girl. Old woman, she smuggle me into Portland. I cost $2500. Don't look it now! Old Chinese man, he took me along to Warrens in pack train."'

One story told that Charlie Bemis won a poker game in the saloon where Polly was working, with Polly as the prize, and a fight broke out between Bemis and half-Indian John Cox. Cox shot Bemis in his right eye. Another, similar version said that Polly was only in the saloon and not involved in the poker game when the fight began. Both versions tell how Polly took care of Bemis—even after the doctor threw up his hands, collected his fee and left. Through Polly's careful nursing,

ESTHER HOBART MORRIS
PROPONENT OF THE LEGISLATIVE ACT WHICH
IN 1869 GAVE DISTINCTION TO THE TERRITORY OF
WYOMING
AS THE 1ST GOVERNMENT IN THE WORLD TO GRANT
WOMEN EQUAL RIGHTS

Bemis' eye was saved, and eventually she and Charlie were married. As one old timer explained it: 'Well, poker had something to do with it…I guess the fact was that Bemis did get hurt in a poker game, Polly nursed him back to health, and nature and a minister did the rest.'

Wyoming and South Dakota

One of the most important women in United States history came out of a Wyoming boom town called South Pass City. The rush in Wyoming was in the 1860s in South Pass. In 1869 history was made when Mrs Esther Morris, one of the town's leading citizens, got each candidate—Republican and Democrat—to promise that if elected he would introduce a bill giving women the right to vote. Mr WH Bright, the Republican, was elected into the territorial legislature and managed to persuade them to pass Mrs Morris' bill. The women of Wyoming not only could vote, they also could hold public office. South Pass City wasted no time in electing Mrs Morris as its justice of the peace. Although some men rebelled, Mrs Morris was able to establish and exert her authority, properly handling all 40 cases brought before her. South Pass City, though a thriving town like its neighbors Miner's Delight and Atlantic City, lost its inhabitants to gold fever

At left: The Esther Hobart Morris statue at the Capitol Building in Cheyenne, Wyoming (see the text, page 147). _At right:_ The well-preserved main street of South Pass City, Wyoming. _Below:_ A distance shot of same, with antique mining equipment in the foreground. _Above right:_ The ghost town of Miner's Delight, Wyoming.

when General George A Custer found gold in the Black Hills of neighboring South Dakota. Newspaper headlines screamed:

GOLD!!
THE LAND OF PROMISE
Stirring News From The
Black Hills

By 1875 Deadwood, South Dakota was growing into a roaring boom town that welcomed such celebrities as Wild Bill Hickok and Calamity Jane. Calamity Jane was so notorious that in another town, when she was arrested, they had to hold her locked in a shed, away from the male prisoners—for the men's protection! Indeed, if Wild Bill knew that Calamity Jane was buried next to him, he would probably turn over in his grave. Although fiction linked the two, Bill never wanted anything to do with Calamity.

One story about Calamity Jane involved the famous preacher Henry Weston Smith, who usually preached to the prospectors while standing on a box, with a hat for contributions at his feet. Calamity picked up the hat and passed it through the crowd while shouting, 'You sinners, dig down in your pokes now; this old fellow looks as though he were broke and I want to collect about 200 dollars for him.' When Smith was killed by Indians on his way to Crook City, Calamity was understandably upset, saying, 'Ain't it too bad the Indians killed the only man that came into the Hills to tell us how to live. And we sure need the telling.'

Within its first year, 1875, Deadwood had 25,000 people crowded together, scrambling for gold. In time, the gold boom died down but Deadwood didn't itself die away like so many other towns. Perhaps it really was 'too tough to die,' retaining 2500 inhabitants into the 1980s.

Wild Bill Hickok *(at left)* was killed in Deadwood, South Dakota, while holding 'aces & eights,' the famous 'dead man's hand.' That he had friends is evidenced by the tombstone and marker at *below left.* Calamity Jane *(below)* was another famous Deadwood resident. *At right:* Diggings in Deadwood, in the 1870s.

Women of the Gold Camps

The women of the gold rushes, whether in California, Alaska, or Montana, were not all the stereotypic madam with the heart of gold nor all the supportive pioneer wife. They were of every type and temperament, of every color and creed. Many arrived with their husbands. Some arrived with only their children, and some arrived alone. Although some were not in the best of health, almost all had the strength of character that allowed them to survive the rigorous life that the boom towns entailed.

Women could do many things in the gold rush era. It was no wonder that it was during the Wyoming rush that women first received the right to vote and to hold public office. Women could do or be nearly anything they wanted. Abby T Mansur's letters home were clear indicators of the morals of the times. On 12 September 1852 she wrote from Horseshoe Bar, Miner's Ravine, California:

'Dear sister it waz with much Joy i received your letter last evening you cannot imagein what pleasure it give me to learn you was all alive and in good health i cannot say that i am well yet but i am a great deal better than i was when i wrote you last i had rather a sick spell after i wrote you before…i do not know but i shall do as Mrs French has i suppose you have not heard how that is she has left French and gone to the city boarding out for her health i espect every day when she will come home for she started for there when she left but the captain would not let her go for she had not money she thought when she left French that he would carry her home for nothing they fell in love with each other comeing out here or he made her believe that he was in love with her and she loved him all most to death and left French for him as near as i can find out and he would not have anything to say to her when she got to the city and so she had to stop there but keep mum you will here about it i think likely…'

On 28 May 1853 Abby again wrote to her sister, saying: '…i tell you the woman are in great demand in this country no matter whether they are married or not you need not think strange if you see me coming home with some good looking man some of these times with a pocket full of rocks you may rest assured that i shall not take up with no common stalk it is all the go here for Ladys to leave there Husbands two out of three do it there is a first rate Chance for a single woman she can have her choice of thousands i wish mother was here she could marry a rich man and not have to lift her hand to do her work…'

A later letter again followed the fortunes of Abby and her husband and the busy life of Mrs French: '…Mrs French is in san Francisco and has been ever since she left French she had had a baby and hires a Dutch woman to take care of it or the man she lives with does she is liveing with a man that is married and has a wife and 4 children at home that is the way the men do here she was stopping first with one man and then with another when she first left French but when she got in family way she had to stop it and since she had her baby she has been living with this man…'

Abby's story did not have a happy ending. She was lonely and homesick, and her health did not allow her to open a boarding house or laundry like many other women did. She did find contentment as the conditions in Horseshoe Bar improved but sadly, she died of heart trouble and exhaustion before she could really enjoy her improved circumstances.

'Woman's work' was a necessity in the gold camps. Someone had to cook, mend clothing and nurse the sick men. Most of the prospectors were too busy at their claims to take care of the day-to-day chores. One woman in Placerville took in washing and, when her own husband came dragging in after a hard day of mining, she laughed at his meager earnings. She was charging all the market could bear and had made more in a few hard hours than her man had made all day.

Some women, however, did not have such good lives, spending their time in the saloons and brothels, little more than slaves. Some escaped that life, while others manipulated the men around them and made their own fortunes. Dainty Lou of Dawson City, Yukon Territory was one mercenary example while the famous Kate Rockwell was another. Kate was the 'Queen of the Klondike,' the last of

the Gold Rush girls. She later recalled those days, saying, 'Dawson, in 1901, was the hilarious heart of the rich gold country. To its theaters and dance halls the miners came for relief from the long, lonely hours on their claims. They laughed, drank, and threw their gold dust recklessly about. I was queen of all that laughter and gaiety! There were whistles and cheers when I appeared on the street, or drove my team through town.'

But not all the women were married or dance hall girls. Mollie Walsh ran a roadhouse in 1897–1898 on the Dead Horse Trail for prospectors on their way to the Yukon. Highly regarded for high morals, her business could compare to Mrs Pullen's, the only safe boarding house in Skagway for some time. Honesty, good morals, and very high standards earned these women the respect of the rough men they encountered in the boom towns.

Finally, there were those women who found their wealth in their prospector husbands. The newspapers carried many 'personals' and each woman had her choice of at least 50 men. One would hope that the right miner saw this ad in his lonely cabin: 'A Husband Wanted—by a lady who can wash, cook, scour, sew, mild, spin, weave, hoe (can't plow), cut wood, make fires, feed the pigs, raise chickens, rock the cradle (but no gold-rocker, I thank you, Sir), saw a plank, drive a nail, etc...She is neither handsome nor a fright; yet an old man need not apply, nor any without education. Gold? There must be 20,000 dollars settled on her before she will bind herself to perform all the above. Address your reply to Dorothy Scraggs, Post Office, Marysville, giving your real name.'

The odds were quite good that Dorothy found her man and, hopefully, happiness as the boom towns began to fade. Wealth had flowed like water from the miners' hands but those days were ending and the women endured the transition as they always had; they made a place for themselves in the West which lasted longer than any material wealth could have. They made the West their home.

Below: **This is a classic frontier family picture, with Pa and his tools and lunch about ready to go down to the diggin's, Ma in her rocking chair on the porch and little Mary Jane just taking it all in. Women brought the possibility of civilized life to the gold camps.**

Montana

It has been said that Montana Territory in the 1860s was full of the dregs of the West, with every badman, outlaw, drifter and unlucky prospector that hadn't already found himself at the wrong end of a noose somehow finding his way to the territory.

Bannack

Montana's first boom town of the 1860s was Grasshopper Diggings, which soon became known as Bannack. Bannack grew quickly but even richer mines were found at Alder Gulch, attracting many miners to build newer boom camps. Bannack, however, retained sufficient prestige to be made the temporary capital of the Idaho Territories, although there was only one legislative meeting before the capital was moved to Alder Gulch.

Being the first territorial capital, even for a short time, was not Bannack's key to fame—or perhaps the word is infamy. Bannack was the headquarters for the most infamous, brazen group of outlaws that ever roamed the western territories. Henry Plummer, the leader of the gang, was an outlaw who had fled from the camps of Nevada and California, been the marshall of Nevada City, California, and later was elected town sheriff. Those men who watched carefully knew that, secretly, Plummer and his men were the outlaws terrorizing local roads, but prudent men said nothing or they might be the next to be found dead or simply 'disappear.'

Plummer claimed that he was often called out of town to look at silver ore samples because he'd gained experience doing this while living in Nevada. Few suspected that the silver had very little to do with his little 'trips.' In reality, he was going to join his gang to commit robberies. Worse, after Plummer had been made sheriff of Bannack, he then used threats and coercion to also be appointed sheriff of Virginia City. This circumstance allowed him to appoint his outlaws as deputies of both towns.

Plummer's reign began to fail after one particular atrocity: the outlaws murdered Lloyd Magruder and his companions, leaving their bodies for the coyotes. Exasperated citizens banded together to form a vigilante committee. It was commonly felt that the situation was a matter of 'kill or be killed.' Twenty-four men gathered together in a motley group, carrying revolvers, rifles, shotguns, blankets and a rope. On 23 December 1863, the first of the vigilante groups set out, enduring snow and bitter cold. They met Erastus 'Red' Yager along the way, not knowing that he was the gang's message carrier. Red lied to the vigilantes about the drunken condition of the Plummer gang and, because of this and a quick trip to warn the gang, they escaped the posse.

Only a few days later, the vigilantes caught up to Yager. He was 'perfectly unconcerned; he was as iron-nerved a man as ever leveled a shotgun at a coach.' He asked no questions, believing (correctly) that his fate was sealed. On the way to Virginia City they also captured GW Brown, the gang's secretary. After comparing the stories of Brown and Yager, the vigilantes voted unanimously on their guilt, then took the two to town to finish the job. Before the execution, Red calmly informed them of the entire gang's activities, the members' names, and most importantly, the identity of the leader. 'On the road to the gallows Red was cool, calm and collected.' The same could not be said for his companion, Brown. Brown's last words were, 'God Almighty, save my soul.' Red watched as his companion dropped, then spoke to the vigilantes, asking that they would punish the rest of the gang and insist-

***Below left:* Bannack, Montana, in the early 1950s. *Below:* The old stagecoach still awaits its passengers in *Montana's* Virginia City. *At bottom, below:* The Bannack jail, in 1953. The notorious Henry Plummer and his gang might have had a chance to reside here if they'd have survived the vigilantes! Bannack had such amenities as the Hotel Meade *(at right)*, and is now a carefully-preserved historical site.**

ing on shaking hands with them all. 'Good-by, boys. God bless you. You are on a good undertaking,' were reported to be the last words he spoke before the rope stretched him.

The bodies were left hanging for some days before they were taken down and buried. The message was plain to the rest of the outlaws, and one by one they were captured. Plummer himself was caught while undressing in his own home. On the way to the gallows, he was joined by Buck Stinson and Ned Ray. Professor Thomas J Dimsdale wrote in *The Vigilantes of Montana* : 'The news of a man's being hanged flies faster than any other intelligence in a Western county, and several had gathered round the gallows on that fatal Sabbath evening—many of them friends of the road agents. The spectators were allowed to come up to a certain point, and were then halted by the guard, who refused permission either to depart or to approach nearer than the "dead line," on the pain of their being instantly shot. The weather was intensely cold, but the party stood for a long time round the bodies of the suspended malefactors, determined that rescue should be impossible. Soon after, the party formed and returned to town, leaving the corpses stiffening in the icy blast. The bodies were eventually cut down by the friends of the road agents and buried. The "Reign of Terror" in Bannack was over.'

The executions followed, one after another, as the outlaws were captured by the vigilantes. It seemed that the end of the lawless gang was near when one of the vigilantes made his own fatal error. JA Slade was a vigilante who often boasted of his membership but was notorious for killing several men in other towns. He was so mean that if there was a problem with the stage—whether it was with highwaymen or poor management—Slade was sent out to take care of it in his usual violent manner. The stagecoach always went through with Slade.

On this final occasion, Slade had let the bottle take control of his vile temper and, after he tore up the town all night, the sheriff arrested him and took him to court to read the warrant. Slade became furious and snatched the paper, shredding it, throwing it on the floor and stomping on it. His companions backed him up by cocking their pistols. The sheriff, being a prudent man, made a cautious exit and notified the vigilantes. Slade had already been warned several times and this was the final declaration of war.

When Slade realized the consequences of this latest episode he attempted to apologize for his behavior to all the parties he had offended, threatened and abused the day before, but it was already too late. The vigilante committee did not want to act against one of its own, but public opinion demanded Slade be punished like any other danger to society. His friends begged and cried for his life but could take no action against the overwhelming odds. Slade met his end, ignomiously, at the end of a rope just like the criminals that he had helped bring to justice.

Millions in gold had traveled the roads of Montana—some taken by the outlaws of Plummer's gang, some making it through the stage routes to make the miners millionaires. Whether the gold came from Alder Gulch, Virginia City or Bannack was unimportant—it was gold and that was good enough for the prospectors.

North of Virginia City many more towns grew up. Garnet, Elkhorn, Granite—the names of many camps were similar to those of the boom towns of California, Nevada and the other western states. But each town had its own story, its own infamous characters and its own method of dying. Whether the prospectors were drawn by stories of better, larger, richer strikes; whether the gold ran out, leaving no reason to stay; whether fires or avalanches or flood overwhelmed the camps; or whether time itself eroded the population, most of the camps shared the common characteristic of eventually becoming ghost towns. Some remain as little more than ruins, others vanished completely and a few, like Bannack and Garnet, are maintained as parks or historic monuments to Montana's Gold Rush days.

At left, in box: The violent vigilante Jack Slade was 'bandit bane,' but was also the bane of law-abiding folks when drunk. They hung Jack after his last wild spree. *Below left:* The grave sites, near Bannack, of Henry Plummer's gang, who had terrorized the Montana mining country, and met their fates in true Montana Gold Country fashion (see the text, pages 152–154). These Montana historical sites also await your visit: *above*, Elkhorn; *at right*, Flathead Lake; and *below*, Monida.

Biographical Notices of the Leading Road Agents of Plummer's Band and Others, from *Vigilantes of Montana* by Professor Thomas J Dimsdale

'Henry Plummer, the chief of the road agent band, the narrative of whose deeds of blood has formed the ground-work of this history, emigrated to California in 1852. The most contradictory accounts of his place of birth and the scene of his early days are afloat; upwards of 20 different versions have been recommended to the author of this work, each claiming to be the only true one. The most probable is that he came to the West from Wisconsin. Many believe he was from Boston, originally; others declare that he was an Englishman by birth, and came to America when quite young. Be this as it may, it is certain, according to the testimony of one of his partners in business, that in company with Henry Hyer, he opened the "Empire Bakery," in Nevada City, California, in 1853.

'Plummer was a man of most insinuating address and gentlemanly manners under ordinary circumstances, and had the art of ingratiating himself with men and even with ladies and women of all conditions. Wherever he dwelt, victims and mistresses of this wily seducer were to be found. It was only when excited by passion that the savage instincts got the better of him and that he appeared—in his true colors—a very demon. In 1856 or 1857, he was elected marshal of the city of Nevada, and had many enthusiastic friends. He was re-elected and received the nomination of the Democratic party for the assembly near the close of his term of office; but as he raised a great commotion by his boisterous demeanor, caused by his success, they threw him off, and elected another man.

'Before the expiration of his official year, he murdered a German named Vedder, with whose wife he had an intrigue. He was one day prosecuting his illicit amours, when Vedder came home, and on hearing his footsteps, he went out and ordered him back. As the unfortunate man continued his approach, he shot him dead. For this offense, Plummer was arrested and tried, first in Nevada, where he was convicted and sentenced to 10 years in the penitentiary; and second, in Yuba County, on a rehearing with a change of venue. Here the verdict was confirmed and he was sent to prison.

'After several months' confinement his friends petitioned for his release on the alleged ground that he was consumptive, and he was discharged with a pardon signed by Governor P Weller. He then returned to Nevada, and joined again with Hyer & Co in the "Lafayette Bakery."

'He soon made a bargain with a man named Thompson, that the latter should run for the office of city marshal, and if successful, that he should resign in Plummer's favor. The arrangement became public and Thompson was defeated.

'Shortly after this, Plummer got into a difficulty in a house of ill-fame with a man from San Juan, and struck him heavily on the head with his pistol. The poor fellow recovered, apparently, but died about a year and a half afterward from the effect of the blow, according to the testimony of the physician.

'...Plummer went over to Washoe and joining a gang of road agents, he was present at the attack on Wells & Fargo's bullion express. He leveled his piece at the driver, but the barrel fell off the stock, the key being out, and the driver, lashing his horses into full speed, escaped.

'He stood his trial for this, and for want of legal proof, was acquitted. He then returned to Nevada City. His next "difficulty" occurred in another brothel where he lived with a young woman as his mistress, and quarreled with a man named Ryder, who kept a prostitute in the same dwelling. 'This victim he killed with a revolver. He was quickly arrested and lodged in the county jail of Nevada. It is more than supposed that he bribed his jailer to assist him in breaking jail. Hitherto, he had tried force; but in this case fraud succeeded. He walked out in open day. The man in charge, who relieved another who had gone to breakfast, declared that he could not stop him, for he had a loaded pistol in each hand when he escaped.

'The next news was that a desperado named Mayfield had killed Sheriff Blackburn, who had dared to arrest him, by stabbing him in the heart with his knife. Of course Mayfield was immediately taken into custody, and Plummer, who had lain concealed for some time, assisted him to get out of jail, and the two started for Oregon in company. To prevent pursuit, he sent word to the California papers that he and his comrade had been hanged in Washington Territory, by the citizens, for the murder of two men.

'All that he accomplished in Walla Walla was the seduction of a man's wife. He joined himself in Idaho to Talbert, alias Cherokee Bob, who was killed at Florence, on account of his connection with

this seduction. Plummer stole a horse and went on the road. In a short time he appeared in Lewiston, and after a week's stay he proceeded with a man named Ridgeley, to Orofino, where he and his party signalized their arrival by the murder of the owner of the dancing saloon during a quarrel. The desperado chief then started for the Missouri, with the intention of making a trip to the States. The remainder of his career has been already narrated, and surely it must be admitted that this "perfect gentleman" had labored hard for the death on the gallows which he received at Bannack, on the 10th of January, 1864.

'As one instance of the many little incidents that so often change a man's destiny, it should be related that when Plummer sold out of the United States Bakery to Louis Dreifus, he had plenty of money and started to San Francisco, intending to return to the East. It is supposed that his infatuation for a Mexican courtesan induced him to forego his design and return to Nevada City. But for this trifling interruption, he might never have seen Montana, or died a felon's death. The mission of Delilah is generally the same, whether her abode is the vale of Sorek or the Rocky Mountains.'

Below left: The State of Montana sponsors tours of Bannack, which was the home base of both the notorious Plummer Gang and of wild Jack Slade. Here, a father and son queue for the tour at the Hotel Meade. _Below:_ Henry Plummer's own grave, with Bannack in the background. _At right:_ The main street of historic Bannack, Montana.

Across the Continent

Not all of America's ghost towns were the results of Western gold rushes. The mass migrations that followed the Civil War left many ghost towns in the East as well. There were places like Eldora, Louisiana, which died around 1888 when the post office moved to another town. Surely the population was already drifting away, but with no post office Eldora's fate was sealed. Rosewood, Florida, whose entire population was black, processed turpentine and was therefore dependent on the lumber industry. When it was burnt to the ground, it was rumored that the KKK had a hand in its demise, but, as the story goes, no one who valued his life investigated the cause too closely.

Roslyn, Washington

The rise of the railroads that was a boon to many cities spelled an end to others. The railroad required steel, lumber and coal, and these raw materials came from both coasts. The workers needed food, shelter and all the other basic requirements of life while they were building the railroads, so towns sprang up to accommodate them and vanished when the tracks had been laid. In 1886 there was a coal rush in Washington state because of the Northern Pacific Railroad. Coal had been discovered in 1883 only four miles from the main line, but it took three years for the railroad to get around to sending its experts. The result was an almost instant town, named Roslyn after someone's hometown in Delaware. By December 1886, three month old Roslyn was forced to expand to make room for new arrivals who were coming from Europe and from throughout the Americas. Over four hundred men—both black and white—crammed into the camp during that first winter.

Being a Northern Pacific-owned 'company town,' Roslyn avoided many of the excesses of the gold towns. The Northern Pacific prohibited gambling dens and controlled the saloon. Of course, other saloons sprang up nearby on private land. When rumors arose about several men having been 'rolled' and left in the woods, the Northern Pacific was forced to relax its restrictions on saloons within the city limits. It was better, they felt, to have their employees in town and roaring drunk than lying in the forest with cracked skulls.

Roslyn flourished even though a fire in 1888 destroyed most of its buildings. Because the railroad needed coal and the coal miners needed

EUROPEAN AGENCY

OF THE

Northern Pacific Railroad,

No. 20 WATER STREET,

LIVERPOOL.

A. ROEDELHEIMER, Agent.

Full and accurate information furnished concerning lands, prices, cost of travel, and openings for farmers, mechanics, tradesmen and, laboreıs in the New American Northwest.

Illustrated Pamphlets, Circulars and Maps sent free to all parts of Europe on application by post to the Agent.

All persons who contemplate emigrating to America should address

A. ROEDELHEIMER,

20 Water Street, Liverpool, England.

Above: **A nineteenth century handbill inviting Europeans to settle along the route of the Northern Pacific Railroad. Lumber towns also sprang up with the North American lumber booms of the nineteenth century; lumberjacks *(at right)* needed food, supplies and amenities, and the wood had to be milled and shipped.**

a place to live, Roslyn was rebuilt. Only one month after the fire, however, labor unions invaded the town. Called the Knights of Labor, the organization organized most of the miners, then called a strike. Actually, the low wages, ten-hour days and hazardous working conditions all were legitimate grievances, and there was a long and bloody strike. Many black crews were imported as strike breakers, and they remained long after the strike was over to form a large part of Roslyn's population. Once the strike was settled, the town went through many hard times. Eventually, a new mine was opened and Roslyn acquired a 'brother' town, Ronald. In time the two towns became privately owned after Congress passed legislation forcing the railroad to sell its mines. Plagued by explosions, the mines began to decline. Also, the railroads slowly began to convert to diesel fuel and the demand for coal dwindled. Much of the town's population moved on, leaving only about 900 permanent residents in the 1980s.

Madrid, New Mexico

Madrid, New Mexico shared a similar fate. Coal mines were opened by the Atchinson, Topeka & Santa Fe Railroad in the early 1880s and the town was quickly built to house the miners. The Santa Fe had no time to waste so they took houses that were in Kansas, cut them in quarters and shipped them to New Mexico where they were reassembled. They were plastered to keep the wind out but somehow the southwestern winds always found their way through the cracks.

Like Roslyn, Madrid was highly regulated by the railroad. When electricity was installed in the houses the light consisted of a single bare bulb hanging in the middle of a room, with the power turned on only during certain night hours. Power for ironing was available—one day a week. However, life did improve in Madrid in the early 1900s. Through the efforts of Oscar Huber, the new mine superintendent, Madrid began to literally blossom. He had water piped into the houses, had schools and a hospital built, and allowed *unlimited* electricity for everyone. Beginning in the 1930s, he even helped the townspeople put on a spectacular Christmas display. Mary, Joseph and Baby Jesus were all created, along with shepherds, wise men and angels. These huge figures were set on a hill overlooking the town in a spectacularly lit Nativity scene that included live animals. This Christmas show brought thousands of visitors to Madrid from early December until New Year. All this faded, however, when the railroad phased coal out. A temporary revival did occur during World War II when 20,000 tons of coal was shipped to Los Alamos. The last Christmas pageant, however, was held in 1941, after which the lights were shut off as a World War II conservation measure.

Los Cerrillos, New Mexico

The Santa Fe Railroad was the spark that brought many towns to life, and it also sparked growth in other towns that were already functioning. Los Cerrillos, New Mexico, for example, had been well known for hundreds of years. The diggings in the 'little hills' were ancient, begun in perhaps 500 AD when the Basket Maker Indians mined there. Later, the Spanish assayed gold and silver ores from the same location, but the Indians drove the Spaniards away and it was another 300 years, in 1879, before the precious metals and turquoise were rediscovered by American prospectors. A small boom brought about 300 men into the area but it took the Santa Fe Railroad to bring the men gushing in. Not only did Los Cerrillos flourish, but smaller towns like Bonanza and Carbonateville sprang up. Then money came in to reopen the Indians' turquoise mines and by 1899 New Mexico was providing over $1.5 million worth of turquoise annually. Time passed and the mines began to fade but Los Cerrillos kept on until neighboring Madrid was abandoned. When the Santa Fe Railroad no longer needed coal, however, both towns withered.

Opal, Wyoming

Another railroad town was Opal, Wyoming. As the Union Pacific Railroad built its rails west from Cheyenne, the usual camps followed to take care of all the construction workers' needs. Most of these 'hell-on-wheels' camps disappeared when the tracks moved forward but a few did linger, the people founding various businesses like shipping from nearby coal fields or oil deposits.

Opal was located on the Utah & Northern Railroad's narrow gauge line that led through the oil and coal fields to its connection with the Union Pacific. Later called the Oregon Short Line, it was finally consolidated with the larger railroad. Opal became one of the railroad towns because it was a good watering place on Ham's Fork of Green River. A flourishing shipping point for livestock, one article in the *Cheyenne Daily Leader* of 10 July 1895 read:

'...Scattered on either side of a heavy upgrade of the Union Pacific tracks, leading from a canyon of the Uinta Mountains of Wyoming, are some half a dozen log houses, a saloon and as many corrals. This is Opal. It seems the height of impudence, writes a tenderfoot correspondent of the *Philadelphia Inquirer*, that a town so limited in its proportions should occupy a place on the map, but Opal is an important city.

'Opal, with its half dozen houses is a metropolis. It is a railroad cen-

Railroads got into hauling coal, lumber and oil; and towns sprang up and died, sprang up and died—and so on! ***At right:*** **Lumber and ore in Eureka, California.** ***Above opposite:*** **An early coal mine.**

ter for a district covering 200 miles to the north, embracing a region of sheep and cattle ranches among the wealthiest in Wyoming and the newly discovered gold mines at Cora, the hope of thousands of speculators and miners…'

'In a business way this little town near the Utah line of Wyoming is an example of western push and enterprise. Each year more than 10,000 cattle are shipped to Chicago, as many sheep and one quarter of a million pounds of wool to Philadelphia and other eastern markets. In return supplies for the hundreds of ranches in the north country are sent here for distribution, and about the little station there is always a burly crowd of teamsters as there is at the Broadway Depot, even if the number is smaller and of a different kind. Altogether, Opal is a typical western city, a place where the chase after the almighty dollar supercedes the chase after the soft and scented anise-seed bag as a form of entertainment, and the possession of gold is the one ambition of every man's life.'

Such places existed all over the continent. In Pennsylvania and Alberta, Canada, there were oil well towns like the aptly-named Oil City, but when the wells dried up, the people moved on and only ruins remain. The railroads' change from coal to diesel motive power in turn spurred the decline of the coal towns. The end of an era was nearing and coal towns like Waldo, British Columbia, Sego, Utah and Crested Butte, Colorado were feeling the cold breath of change. The nation was changing, technology was evolving rapidly and many of the products that kept the old town booming simply were no longer needed. Who else would buy the vast piles of coal when the railroad no longer wanted them? What would happen to the men who had spent their lives in the forest and mines? Though World War I would spur some mines to reopen, they would not go on forever.

The Second Gold Rush

Tonopah, Nevada

'Lazy' Jim Butler was looking for his burros on 19 May 1900 when he found an outcropping on a ledge near a hidden spring called Tonopah for the plants growing there. Lazy Jim was in no hurry. He went on and met some other prospectors who were making a few dollars off their claims. He couldn't convince them to assay his samples so he trudged on back to Tonopah and took a few more samples and had his friend, Tasker L Oddie, arrange for an assay.

Luckily, Lazy Jim had not bothered to mark the outcropping at Tonopah. This proved to be fortunate for him because the rumor moved faster than he did in returning to his claim. Prospectors passed by the ledge without a second glance and Jim's strike was saved until he returned. The western economy had slumped significantly since the Comstock Lode had played out 20 years before, but now, after losing at least a third of its population, Nevada had a new strike. Tonopah, however, survived into the present, while the boom towns spawned by the Second Gold Rush faded and died.

Tonopah was known all over the country, generating as much excitement as the Mother Lode or the Comstock strikes. Men poured into Nevada from every part of the country. Some enterprising locals soon found a way to earn food or liquor money without working. They'd wander up to a stranger with a likely looking bit of ore in hand and ask, 'What do you think 'bout this piece of rock?' Often they'd get some money which they'd drink up without ever setting foot outside of town. If they did get supplies they'd go out into the desert for a few days.

One of these men was a Shoshone Indian, Tom Fisherman. One day he brought in a different specimen than his usual samples. He showed it to Tom Kendall at the Tonopah Club, who gave Fisherman $10 to go stake the ground. Fisherman got drunk instead. All they could get out of him was that he'd picked up the float 'twenty-thirty miles south.'

Billy Marsh and Harry Stimler wanted a grub-stake so Kendall and Jim Butler provided an outfit and suggested they head south. It was only three days before the two young prospectors found gold and named the region the Grandpa.

Above right: **Lazy Jim Butler, who discovered the big Tonopah strike, and the mule he had with him when he found it.** ***At right:*** **A 1907 photo of the town of Tonopah, which had grown phenomenally with the new strike: the town stretches out of sight.** ***Opposite:*** **An antique utility pole at Rhyolite, Nevada, shows the way to Tonopah.**

WIN WITH
WILLKIE
BEATTY 4
TONOPAH 100
WATER 10
FURNACE CREEK RANCH 38
AUTO CLUB

E.W. SMITH
PHOTO.
WORKMEN SUPPLY THEIR OWN BEDING
BUT ARE FURNISED SPACIOUS AIRY BED ROOMS.

T&N.O.
9826

Below: The Mohawk gold mine, in Goldfield, New Mexico. Towns of the turn of the century gold strikes tended to grow fast and fade fast, in direct proportion to the gold supply. Mines like this one were often subject to 'highgrading'—*ie*, miners taking ore for themselves while they were mining for the company. This photo was taken in the first decade of our century. Goldfield itself was founded in 1903.

At far left: A jokester supplied his own caption to this 1904 photo of the miners' open-air sleeping quarters. *At left:* Gold ore sacked for shipment at the Combination mine near Goldfield, in 1903. *At right:* Goldfield's second saloon, 'The Combination,' owned and run by Ole Elliott.

Although the gold ore already constituted one-sixth of the value of Tonopah, a few men believed that more gold was out there. On 23 May 1903 Al Myers and Bob Hart staked their claim about three miles from Marsh and Stimler's claims. The new claim paid off, becoming the Combination Mine.

Goldfield, Nevada

Tonopah was experiencing an unemployment problem and the Grandpa was discovered because the lack of jobs in town led the men out into the desert, and also on to the founding of Goldfield in the fall of 1903.

'Thar's gold in them thar hills' echoed throughout the country and it wasn't long before Goldfield was a booming camp. At a time when there was so much gold in the mines the workers often just helped themselves, illegally carrying out hundreds of dollars in ore. Soon special jackets were developed which had pockets from shoulders to the hem. These 'corset covers' could even be bought in stores like regular equipment. Some men carried out so much gold in this manner that they could hardly walk, yet mine foremen never seemed to see them. It was said that men actually bought their $5 a day jobs, paying $20 a day, in order to 'highgrade' the gold as the Colorado miners had done 20 years before.

As always, any crime that could inspire a good laugh was not always necessarily punished in Goldfield, and one prime example was a robbery at one of the big saloons. The roulette wheel was always locked in a floor box at night to prevent tampering. During working hours that same box was used as a safe, with a chair and a lookout seated upon it, so that no one could get in. A man named 'Jackass Slim' who had lost a lot of money on the wheel figured out a way to recoup his losses. He surveyed where the money box was located and dug a tunnel under the saloon where he cut a 12-inch square hole in the bottom of the box so that the next deposit literally dropped into his hands. However, the dealer and the lookout man heard a sound they couldn't identify and quickly came to the same conclusion. Throwing open the box, they found only the hole, so they leaped up and ran to the back of the saloon

At right: **The old railroad station in the mining town of Rhyolite, on the Nevada end of Death Valley, sometime in the early 1900s.** ***Below:*** **Another view of Rhyolite as it was in more recent times. The boom came and went, and so did the populace.**

RHYOLITE

where Jackass Slim crawled out of his tunnel right into the arms of a reception committee! His jaw dropped as the crowd roared with laughter, which was enough punishment. The next day his wages were welcomed as usual when he arrived to gamble them away.

Goldfield was rich and growing but there was not enough room for all the prospectors streaming in from every direction, searching for new claims. Among the better new strikes spawned the towns of Rhyolite and Bullfrog. Rhyolite sprang up near the very rich Montgomery-Shoshone Mine and 'Old Man' Beatty's spring, which in turn became the contemporary town of Beatty. At first, Rhyolite promised to become a permanent settlement, with all the rich investors and prospectors pouring in. Still, the boom didn't last long. In 1907 Tex Rickard, a publicity man, spread across the front of an empty church in Goldfield a huge sign that read: *This Church Is Closed. God Has Gone To Rawhide.*

Rawhide, Nevada

Everyone had a good laugh and followed. Another financial panic had struck and, in 1907, Rawhide promised employment and another chance at riches beyond belief. As Zeb Kendall, a successful operator in Tonopah and Goldfield, put it 23 years later, 'Yes, Rawhide was a great camp—for a minute. In three months we went to ten thousand population, and in three months more back to nothing.'

Though not quite accurate, Kendall's assessment of Rawhide was a near enough description of yet another flash-in-the-pan camp. The eulogy of Riley Grannan might well have been that of Rawhide. Delivered by WH Knickerbocker, it symbolized the very heart of the mining camp:

'I feel that it is incumbent upon me to state that in standing here I occupy no ministerial or prelatic position I am simply a prospector. I make no claims whatever to moral merit or religion except the religion of humanity, the brotherhood of man. I stand among you today simply as a man among men, feeling that I can shake hands and say "brother" to the vilest man or woman that ever lived. If there should come to you anything of moral admonition through what I say, it comes not from any sense of moral superiority, but from the depth of my experience.

'Riley Grannan was born in Paris, Kentucky, about 40 years ago. I suppose he dreamed all the dreams of boyhood. They blossomed into phenomenal success along financial lines at times during his life. I am told that from the position of bellboy in a hotel he rose rapidly to be a celebrity of worldwide fame. He was one of the greatest plungers, probably, that the continent has ever produced. He died day before yesterday in Rawhide. This is a very brief statement. You have the birth and the period of the grave. Who can fill in the interim? Who can speak of his hopes and fears? Who can solve the mystery of his quiet hours that only himself knew? I can not...He died in Rawhide, where in winter the shoulders of the mountains are wrapped in garments of ice and in summer the blistering rays of the sun beat down upon the skeleton ribs of the desert...

'He was a man whose exterior was a placid and gentle as I have ever known, and yet when we look back over his meteoric past we can readily understand...that he was absolutely invincible in spirit. If you will allow me I will use a phrase most of you are acquainted with. He was a "dead game sport." I say it not irreverently, but till the phrase as full of practical human philosophy as it will hold, and I believe that when you say one is "a dead game sport" you have reached the climax of human philosophy...

'I know there are those who will condemn him. There are those who believe today that he is reaping the reward of a misspent life. There are those who are dominated by medieval creeds. To those I have no words to say in regard to him. They are ruled by the skeleton hand of the past and fail to see the moral beauty of a character lived outside their own puritanical ideas. His goodness was not of the type that reached its highest manifestations in any ceremonial piety. His goodness, I say, was not of that type, but of the type that finds expression in a word of cheer to a discouraged brother; the type that finds expression in friendship, the sweetest flower that grows along the dusty highway of life; the type that finds expression in manhood.

'As we stand in the presence of death, we have no knowledge, but always, no matter how dark the gloomy clouds hang before me, there gleams the star of hope. Let up hope, then, that it may be the morning star of eternal day. It is dawning somewhere all the time. Did you ever pause to think that this old world of ours is constantly swinging into the dawn? Down the groves of time, flung by the hand of God, with every revolution it is dawning somewhere all the time. Let this be an illustration of our hope. Let us believe, then, that in the development of the human soul, as it swings forward toward its destiny, it is constantly swinging nearer and nearer to the sun.

'And now the time has come to say goodby. The word "farewell" is the saddest in our language. And yet there are sentiments sometimes that refuse to be confined in that word. I will say "Goodby, old man." We will try to exemplify the spirit manifested in your life in bearing the grief of our parting. Words fail me here. Let these flowers, Riley, with their petaled lips and perfumed breath, speak in beauty and fragrance the sentiments that are too tender for words. Goodby.'

Thus, the eulogy served as a the symbol of not only the man, Riley Grannan, but his home, Rawhide. Although in death he lay peaceful and quiet, in life he made many mistakes. These did not mean he was a 'bad' man, only that he, too, was human. Rawhide suffered the same fate as the man. Cut short in its prime, the town also lived a life of imperfection, hard and fast, yet part of the brotherhood of the miners and their homes. The spirits that move men to great good and great evil, lived in Rawhide as well as in Riley Grannan.

None know what the future will bring. One can only hope that the new day will shine on a better and brighter world. Today, Riley and Rawhide share that same fate, that same vision of eternal peace that lingers in the vastness of the Nevada desert.

The Depression and Prohibition

It was the eve of the Great Depression in March 1927 when the 'mail-order prospectors' arrived in Weepah, Nevada, complete with new boots, fleece-lined sleeping bags and new Ford motor cars. Of course Weepah's boom promptly collapsed.

Prohibition was in full force when such old mining camps as Campo Seco soon found a new enterprise—moonshining. When quitting time

Below: **The desert sun beats down on the ruins of a once-elegant building, in the ghost town that is Rhyolite, Nevada.** ***Above near right:*** **Tourists, horses and power lines: Rawhide, Nevada has become a monument to days gone by.** ***Above far right:*** **Miners and cowpunchers at Weepah, Nevada, in 1927.** ***At right:*** **Campo Seco in the 1950s.**

One of numerous 'speakeasy' resorts that sprang up during the Prohibition Era, Drawbridge, California, died when alcholic beverages were legalized. *At left:* The lonely vistas stretch forth from the faded elegance of this Drawbridge public house.

Located by the San Francisco Bay, Drawbridge has many standing structures *(above)* remaining; the time for taking photos may not be long, however, as some of its buildings are already sinking *(below)* in the marshy Bay flatlands.

came the men were not interested in 'near-beer.' A still and shop were set up in a stone building and once again times were good in Campo Seco. The illegal bar was never raided by federal agents and business flourished. Prudently, when the claim finished, the owners of the building set fire to the wooden interior. They had kept up the insurance premiums and collected on their policy.

Another 'town' of the early 1930s was located right on San Francisco Bay near Alviso. Known as Drawbridge, it was a refuge of liquor and gambling for those trying to escape the misery of the Depression. It was almost like a resort and one could buy luxuries that the law no longer permitted. Similar places dotted the entire United States. With the repeal of Prohibition these places closed forever.

The Depression brought out the desert rats because, as always, when stocks were down the price of gold rose. Oldtimers began to remember the tales of lost mines, and soon they had convinced themselves that some remote place was certainly the right spot, fitting the vaguely remembered description heard in some saloon or at a campfire 30 years before. In fact, some of these mine stories dated back to 1849 and the first rush to the Mother Lode.

Dreams of these lost treasures led many men out to their deaths. The swings of the economy, the Great Depression and the fantasy of untold wealth brough would-be prospectors from all over the country to again search the mountains and deserts. World War II ended many of these dreams, pulling people into the war effort and providing much-needed jobs. Yet some old mines were revived, just as they had been in World War I.

The invention of the atom bomb spurred the hunt for a new element: uranium. Prospectors roamed the mountains. Towns such as Lajitas, Texas experienced a renewed economic boom. After all, the prospectors had to buy their supplies somewhere.

Lajitas

Lajitas was originally a peaceful village on the banks of the Rio Grande River. The river was shallow and easy to cross at that point. It was a natural place for a trail and a town. The United States stationed troops there to protect the mining camps of the Big Bend area. Both General John J Pershing and Lt General George Patton were stationed at Lajitas before World War I. It was there that the colorful Mexican bandit Pancho Villa was murdered in 1923.

Lajitas survived partially because it was the main importation point for a Mexican plant locally called 'cendelia cactus.' It was a source of wax that supplied about 45 percent of Wrigley's chewing gum needs. In 1949 that boom ended when Mexico put a ban on the exportation of the cactus. Then the search for uranium began. Beyond the need for supplies, the eager prospectors also needed a place to wet their dry throats and tell their tales of almost and might-have-been big strikes. But again, Lajitas faded as the prospectors drifted away. The war had ended and the whole country slipped back into its routine domestic life. The world had left the prospectors behind again.

***Above opposite:* Veteran prospector 'Seldom Seen Slim' builds a claim marker in this 1927 photo. *Opposite:* The light of the present filters into the past at Drawbridge, California. *Above:* Whenever a mineral—be it silver, gold or *uranium*—is in demand, men go prospecting. *Below:* A prospector and his burros.**

North to Alaska and the Yukon

The amazing thing about the gold and silver prospectors of the nineteenth century was how they managed to convince themselves that each new rumor, each new strike was going to be the big one. With the first news of gold in Alaska in April 1858, many prospectors swarmed north. Certainly the thought of gold in frozen Alaska should have been daunting, but the miners headed north without a thought of any consequence except getting rich in the new gold fields. A classic story of the prospectors' faith in rumor was told by CB Glasscock in *Gold In Them Hills*:

'Two prospectors died in the fullness of their years, and contrary to their own expectation and that of their friends found themselves in Heaven. A third, unknown to them, came later to the Gate and was admitted by St Peter with some hesitation.

'"What's the trouble?" the newcomer asked. "You let me in but I don't hear any welcoming chorus."

'"I have let you in," said St Peter. "You've always worked hard for your grub-stakers, and you've worshiped God out under the stars at night, and played fair and haven't told any lies that would do any one any real harm. You are in the Book to be let in, but I must admit that you are not very welcome. I let a couple of prospectors in a while back and they've been a nuisance. They're always tearing up the golden streets."

'"Well," said the newcomer, "I'll fix that. You show me these fellers and I'll get rid of 'em for you."

'And a day or two later the two original prospectors appeared at the Gate and asked to be released. No amount of questioning could get at the reason for their request, but St Peter, having warned them that once out they couldn't come back, agreed cheerfully to let them go.

'All was peace in Heaven for a few days. Then St Peter came upon the third and remaining prospector, seated in thought upon a heap of golden paving stones.

'"You did very well, my good man," he said. "Your friends have gone. How did you arrange it?"

'The prospector grinned. "I just let it drop that there was a rich new strike in Hell," he said.

'But that wasn't all and here is the revelation of the prospector spirit. A few days later the remaining prospector approached St Peter at the Gate. "I'd like to get out," he said.

'"Why? Everything is peaceful and lovely here now since your destructive associates have left. Heaven certainly owes you a debt of thanks. If there is anything we can do to make you happier, you may command me and it will be done."

'"Well, I reckon you'd better let me out. I been thinkin' about that new strike in Hell, an' I believe there's something in it. I'd like to get down there ahead of the rush an' stake me a few good claims."'

Barkerville

Billy Barker was an English sailor in his pre-prospecting career and it is likely that he knew nothing of gold mining. However, when the Canadian wilderness beckoned, Billy jumped ship. He was tough, making his way through wilderness to the Williams Creek Diggings, 70 miles southwest from today's Prince George, British Columbia. No one knows exactly why Billy chose to dig his mine shaft some distance from the creek. Was it because somehow Billy knew where to look for the ancient stream bed? Or was it because other miners had staked the entire Williams Creek area and Billy dug in at the only spot left? In any case, on 13 August 1862 Billy and his partners began to dig. At 35 feet some wanted to quit but they kept on digging. At 50 feet they reached the old river bed, where they struck gold.

To celebrate, the men had to go all the way into Richfield to find a saloon. Once there, however, they didn't have far to look, for soon there were at least half a dozen establishments complete with drinks, dancing girls and card sharps, all busily lightening the prospectors' pokes. Wine, women and song—or maybe it was really whiskey, cards and girls bellowing popular tunes at the lonely miners' request.

Billy Barker really didn't have much of a chance to enjoy his riches. Within a year he'd decided that he could afford a wife and had brought a widow from Victoria to his namesake, Barkerville. Since Billy was bowlegged, bearded, short, stocky and 42 years old, it can be assumed that his new wife had heard of his fantastic wealth before agreeing to this role. Between the saloons and keeping his wife's attention from the younger, more handsome miners, Billy soon ran through all his money and Mrs Barker then abandoned him. Broke, Billy cooked for road crews until constant drinking and a persistent sore on his lip finally made him unemployable. He died of cancer on 11 July 1894 in the Old Men's Home in Victoria.

At right: **The Fraser River, in British Columbia's Gold Country. Men like Billy Barker (see text, above) found gold and had towns named for them in these environs. Gold fever took men up the North American coast to Alaska and the Yukon Territory.**

Even as its founder was slipping toward his demise, Barkerville was booming. It also came to be uniquely adapted to its environment. After the fire of September 1868, it was rebuilt with its building elevated a few feet, since Williams Creek tended to revert to the old river bed which ran under Barkerville whenever the miners made temporary dams. Since street mud was usually knee deep anyway (except in August) the main purpose of elevating the buildings seems to have been to keep water out of the businesses. The *Cariboo Sentinel* of Barkerville was often filled with the news of new gold strikes, terrible weather and near famine. One winter the *Sentinel* reported: 'There is not a pound of beef or mutton to be procured at any of the butchering establishments on the creek. At Richfield, we believe, there is a small quantity of fresh pork that sells at 62 cents a pound, Mr Toomey and Mr Clark are both out after cattle...we will have to betake ourselves to the old fare of earlier times, beans and bacon, for a change...

Uniquely, Barkerville was not known for its violence. The lack of shootings, murders and lynchings can be attributed to the difficulty in getting in and out of the camp. It simply wasn't possible to flee the scene of the crime ahead of the mob, so men thought twice before pulling a gun. The climate and the terrain can therefore be credited with the peace in Barkerville. Soon, the gold in Williams Creek began to pinch out. Men started leaving for new claims on the Peace River. Barkerville began to die. Claims that before could not be bought for any price now could not be sold and were just abandoned.

Skagway

The largest and most famous rush of the Far North was the Klondike Gold Rush of 1898. (The term 'Klondike' came from a mispronunciation of the Indian word 'Trundeck,' a creek known to the American traders as Deer Creek.) The 'Trail of '98' fueled the imagination of later years, especially since it began 50 years after the first western rush and men still remembered participating in that first boom. Its jumping off place was Skagway, Alaska—the last outpost of 'civilization' before the prospectors headed out to Dawson City and beyond. The men and their supplies would be dumped unceremoniously onto the beach from the steamships they'd taken up the coast, and many a Yukon-bound passenger lost his luggage to the high tide. The steamers were only being practical; they couldn't get close enough to the beach to land, so they had to ferry everything across. Any man who wanted to keep all his belongings had to move at top speed to higher ground before the tide rose. If he was unsuccessful, it was nearly impossible to replace anything in Skagway. Almost 800 miles northwest of Barkerville, it was so remote that it was difficult to bring in extra supplies. Even if some enterprising soul had managed to get supplies in, some other man probably would have stolen them.

Below: **Actresses, going to the Klondike, ford the (variously named) Dyea River just south of Skagway, in 1897.** ***At right:*** **A preserved miner's cabin at Rampart, Alaska.** ***Opposite:*** **Modern Gold Rush publicity.** ***Overleaf:*** **Historic Skagway, Alaska.**

KLONDIKE GOLD RUSH
☆NATIONAL HISTORICAL PARK☆
☆☆SKAGWAY, ALASKA☆☆
NOW SHOWING
"DAYS OF ADVENTURE DREAMS OF GOLD"
A 30 MINUTE COLOR TALKING PICTURE SHOW PRESENTED ON THE HOUR
and
"The Klondike Gold Rush"
A 10 MINUTE LANTERN SLIDE SHOW PRESENTED ON THE HALF HOUR
WALKING TOURS
11 a.m. & 3 p.m. Daily
Join a National Park Ranger for a stroll through history along Skagway's boardwalks
RANGER TALK
10 a.m. Daily
Programs with special Gold Rush themes to help you peek into the past
A Program, Of Special Interest! Daily 4 p.m.
Hikers! Be prepared! Check with a Ranger for trail conditions & information
ALL ACTIVITIES AT
VISITOR CENTER
2nd & Broadway
SUMMER HOURS 8AM-6PM

FRONTIER BAR

MAES
SNACK SHACK
GMC

Skagway was not a gold town, it was only the beginning of the trail to the gold fields of the Yukon, and here the 'predators' (both prospector *and* criminal) gathered. Many criminals found their way to the Alaskan territory and found it easy to operate in Skagway. Both prospectors and criminals were trying to make their way to Dawson City, but the Canadian Mounties stood at the top of the pass, refusing to allow known criminals or men without adequate supplies into British Columbia to get through.

One of Skagway's criminals managed to terrorize the town and the trail to the Klondike until he was killed in July 1898. His name was Jefferson Randal Smith but he was known as 'Soapy.' He was reportedly a Southern gentleman with a suave and debonair manner, though cold-blooded as a snake. The nickname 'Soapy' came from his scheme for selling bars of soap on street corners. One package also held a five dollar bill but that was always noisily 'found' by one of Soapy's friends posing as a naive bystander. Hoards of greedy, gullible customers would then line up to buy five cents worth of soap for 50 cents, hoping to find another five dollar bill.

Skagway was ripe for Soapy Smith and his confederates. He bought a saloon and hired an assortment of thieves, thugs, prostitutes and gamblers that he had brought with him from the dying camps of Colorado. To this selection he added local badmen until his gang had about 300 members. (Surely it must have been difficult to split the take, but Soapy must have managed somehow.) An unsuspecting but prosperous-looking steamer passenger would be met, greeted warmly, invited to the hospitality of Skagway and guided to Soapy's Saloon for a free drink. Then the tenderfoot would be introduced to the second lesson of Skagway: a cracked skull, stripped pockets, and being left on the street to fend for himself. Soapy was, of course, never in the vicinity when these incidents occurred. He amused himself by helping widows, orphans and the sick—but these good deeds did not mask his other activities for long.

The citizens of Skagway finally realized that if Soapy weren't stopped, the prospectors would go to Dyea or St Michael instead, and spend their gold dust and nuggets in the other towns. Profits would disappear and that simply wouldn't do. So a mass meeting for the vigilantes was organized in a warehouse at the end of Sylvester Dock.

Smith's spies, however, learned of the meeting and carried the news to him. Criminal or not, Soapy was not a coward. He went to the dock, intending to disrupt the meeting. He was met there by an engineer named Frank H Reid who told him, 'You can't go down there, Smith.'

'Damn you, Reid! You have been at the bottom of all my troubles,' Smith cursed. 'If I had got rid of you three months ago, I would never have had this trouble.'

In the ensuing struggle Reid was shot in the groin but he shot Soapy in the heart. Reid lived for 10 days in agony before he died. His monument read, 'He died for the honor of Skagway.' Of Smith's gang, some were captured and some fled into the mountains, surrendering later when starvation threatened.

But Smith was not the most *famous* person who lived in Skagway. That honor was reserved for a woman—Harriet Smith Pullen, known as 'Ma Pullen,' a widow with four children. She came to Skagway in the summer, ready and willing to work. At first hired as a cook at three

Below: **Gold panning was done in the Yukon just as it was done in Canada and the 'lower Forty-Eight,' as is well-evidenced by these *modern-day* 'sourdoughs.'** ***At right:*** **Before, during and after the Gold Rush: Traditional Native American crafts.**

dollars a day, she was soon making dried apple pies for a dollar each in her off hours. She managed to make enough money to bring her four children home by Christmastime. Ma Pullen also saved enough money to bring her seven horses up to Skagway by steamer. With her horses she was able to run a pack train over White Pass, until a narrow gauge railroad was built over the mountain. She then began a hotel in a house she had bought from a successful pioneer-turned-prospector. It wasn't long before she was one of the most well-known characters in Alaska. Her guests through the years included Robert W Service, Jack London and President Warren G Harding. She never had to pay for advertising; word of mouth sufficed.

Ma Pullen ran the only safe hotel while Soapy reigned over Skagway. It was not recorded whether she and Soapy Smith had ever clashed but it seems doubtful. It has been said that even a hardened criminal would avoid a woman with her mind set to accomplish a particular goal. But even Ma met her match in 'Charlie' Walker.

Ma had hired Charlie to build a fireplace for her hotel and he did a good job. The only problem was that he left one board blocking the flue. When he tried to collect his money, Ma said he'd get it in due time. The first time she lit a fire, the smoke billowed out of the fireplace and her guests scattered in every direction. Furious, she located Charlie. His calm reply must have further infuriated the determined woman. 'Ma—when you pay for the fireplace job it will stop smoking.' Ma paid Charlie and he just pulled the board out of the flue.

Ma Pullen earned her money through hard work, but other women, such as 'Dainty Lou,' found gold in different ways. A dance hall girl, Lou was prettier than many and always had an interest in a well filled 'poke.' Once a miner fell head over heels in love with Lou, but unfortu-

nately 'Dog-Tooth Harry' of Dawson City was aptly named. 'A face only mother could love' was only the beginning in describing how ugly poor Harry was. He wanted to get married but, as legend has it, the girls had to get drunk before they could even look at him.

Harry proposed to Lou repeatedly, but she would laugh and use every opportunity to humiliate him. One day she foolishly announced that she was worth her weight in gold and would sell herself to the man who met her price. Dog-Tooth Harry snatched at this chance. Picking Lou up, he carried her to the nearest store with a scale, where she weighed in at 142 pounds—about $24,500 in then-current dollars. She was furious but her tune changed when Harry brought in his gold. He matched her weight, ounce for ounce. Greed gleamed in her eyes and, throwing her arms around his neck, she said loudly, 'Dog-Tooth Harry, you're the handsomest man in all Dawson City.'

Harry looked at her, removing her hands from his neck. He stuffed the cash money into a pocket and forcefully spat between her feet before stomping back to his claim.

Dainty Lou was not the only woman in Dawson City to try to sell herself to the highest bidder. Another was purchased for a mere $5000, so that the buyer could have company through a long, cold winter. The lady was no fool, however, because the money was held in trust by the Alaska Commercial Company.

The Yukon

The Yukon Territory of Canada was an entirely different situation than the wide open camps of the United States territories. The Royal Canadian Mounted Police did not tolerate the sort of foolishness that came out of the American boom towns. Before a prospector could even *enter* Canada he had to show a ton of supplies. Once a man reached Dawson City, he found that there were really two cities. One was Dawson and the other, across the river, was known as Klondike City or South Dawson. The Mounties forced all the brothels to move to the latter, in a two block row of cabins known as White Chapel. It wasn't long until this entire red-light district was renamed Louse Town because of the tiny vermin that somehow managed to elude the Mounties' dragnets. It was even reported that the men were running races with the lice, and one enterprising fellow who'd bred a faster strain actually offered stud service.

Of the men who didn't spend all their time across the river, many made their fortunes in just a relatively short time. Alex McDonald was a fabulously lucky miner who one day in June 1899 checked his sluice box and found so much gold that he reportedly needed 29 mules to pack it into town. As in California, claims were often abandoned or sold as worthless, to the advantage of the next owner who might dig a little deeper and find a fortune. A few—a very lucky few—found streaks on the bedrock where the gold had washed together into one mass that was more gold than gravel.

Again, as in the United States, digging for gold was not the only way to get rich in the Yukon. Scurvy often threatened the prospectors and an Englishman who had brought in a huge stock of orange marmalade soon found that he could sell the tins for prices that were outrageous even for a gold camp. Another man brought in a string of milk goats. They had helped pull his sled on the difficult trail but they were now also a continuing source of his livelihood. Many of the surplus animals were butchered but these goats were worth their weight in gold because only rancid-tasting canned milk was available in town, fresh milk—even goat's milk—was considered a delicacy.

In 1899 new rumors of gold began drawing prospectors away from Dawson. This stampede was a little different. It wasn't often that gold was found in the sands of a beach! Soon at least 500 men were working on the narrow strip of beach near Nome, Alaska. Within three years this new rush had also ended, the men drifting away from the 'Golden Sands.' A new strike at Fairbanks, Alaska, had beckoned but the gold there was not for the poor prospector. The ground had to be thawed before it could be worked and coal ran $150 a ton. Still, camps sprang up around Fairbanks. Many used dredges to mine the creeks, which were abandoned when the gold ran out.

Certainly there was still gold in the Yukon, but the cost of mining in permafrost compared to the estimated value of the gold didn't allow for a large profit. The easiest gold had already been mined and carried southward by the ton. Yet the rumors persisted that the largest gold fields had not yet been found. Because no one knew for sure, some hearty prospectors kept looking.

Gold mining methods evolved in Alaska, and near Fairbanks—which has much Gold Rush-era historical 'treasure'—tenderfeet may try their hand at old-fashioned panning, or may explore huge 'Goldstream Dredge No 8' ***(at right and overleaf)*****, which dredged the gold deposits of Engineer and Goldstream creeks from 1929–59.**

GOLDSTREAM DR
NO. 8
Fairbanks, Alaska

Robert W Service

Robert W Service, like Mark Twain, Bret Harte and Jack London, found a rich source of material for his work in the boom towns of the great gold rushes. Inspired by the tall tales and wild exaggerations of true stories, these writers found their own 'gold' in the wealth of information and misinformation passed on by the eager prospectors. These tales are often the only remnants of the ghost towns of the Far North, the weather having destroyed the ruins that would have survived in a desert climate.

'The Cremation of Sam McGee' was a tale that was too good for Service to pass by. It seems that the steamer *Olive May* had gotten stuck on the mud flats at the head of Lake Le Barge, north of Whitehorse in Yukon Territory. Caught in the fall freeze-up, the crew was forced to spend the winter aboard the ship. In a nearby cabin an old trapper was seriously ill with scurvy. Dr Sugden went to care for the man but found him dead. The ground was, of course, frozen solid, so with the help of the crew Dr Sugden borrowed the *Olive May*'s firebox and cremated the old man. He later turned the ashes over to the police.

Service was a bank clerk in Whitehorse when he heard the tale from Dr Sugden, who was his roommate. Perhaps they didn't know the name of the old prospector. In any case, Service borrowed the name Sam McGee from a friend and wrote his poem.

Robert Service lived in this cabin *(at bottom, below)*, where he wrote the poem at right. *Below:* Historic Whitehorse, Yukon Territory. *Opposite:* Readying the dog sled for another wilderness trek.

**The Cremation of
Sam McGee**

There are strange things done in the midnight sun
By men who moil for gold;
The Arctic trails have their secret tales
That would make your blood run cold;
The Northern Lights have seen queer sights;
But the queerest they ever did see
Was that night on the marge of Lake Lebarge
I cremated Sam McGee.

Now Sam McGee was from Tennessee, where
the cotton blooms and blows.
Why he left his home in the South to roam
'round the Pole, God only knows.
He was always cold, but the land of gold seemed
to hold him like a spell;
Though he'd often say in his homely way that
'he'd sooner live in hell.'

On a Christmas Day we were mushing our way
over the Dawson trail.
Talk of your cold! through the parka's fold it
stabbed like a driven nail.
If our eyes we'd close, then the lashes froze till
sometimes we couldn't see;
It wasn't much fun, but the only one to whimper
was Sam McGee.

And that very night, as we lay packed tight in
our robes beneath the snow,
And the dogs were fed, and the stars o'erhead
were dancing heel and toe,
He turned to me, and 'Cap,' says he, 'I'll cash
in this trip, I guess;
And if I do, I'm asking you won't refuse my
last request.'

Well, he seemed so low that I couldn't say no;
then he says with a sort of moan:
'It's the cursed cold, and it's got right hold till
I'm chilled clean through to the bone.
Yet 'tain't being dead—it's my awful dread of
the icy grave that pains;
So I want you to swear that, foul or fair, you'll
cremate my last remains.'

A pal's last need is a thing to heed, so I swore
I would not fail;
And we started on at the streak of dawn; but
God! he looked ghastly pale.
He crouched on the sleigh, and he raved all day
of his home in Tennessee;
And before nightfall a corpse was all that was
left of Sam McGee.

Now a promise made is a debt unpaid, and the
    trail has its own stern code.
In the days to come, though my lips were dumb,
    in my heart how I cursed that load.
In the long, long night, by the lone firelight,
    while the huskies, round in a ring,
Howled out their woes to the homeless snows
    —O God! how I loathed the thing.

And every day that quiet clay seemed to heavy'
    and heavier grow
And on I went, though the dogs were spent and
    the grub was getting low;
The trail was bad, and I felt half mad, but I
    swore I would not give in;
And I'd often sing to the hateful thing, and it
    hearkened with a grin.

Till I came to the marge of Lake Lebarge, and
    a derelict there lay;
It was jammed in the ice, but I saw in a trice it
    was called the 'Alice May.'
And I looked at it, and I though a bit, and I
    looked at my frozen chum;
Then 'Here,' said I, with a sudden cry, 'is
    my cre-ma-tor-eum.'

Some planks I tore from the cabin floor, and I
    lit the boiler fire;
Some coal I found that was lying around, and I
    heaped the fuel higher;
The flames just soared, and the furnace roared
    —such a blaze you seldom see;
And I burrowed a hole in the flowing coal, and
    I stuffed in Sam McGee.

Then I made a hike, for I didn't like to hear him
    sizzle so;
And the heavens scowled, and the huskies
    howled, and the wind began to blow.
It was icy cold, but the hot sweat rolled down my
    cheeks, and I don't know why;
And the greasy smoke in an inky cloak went
    streaking down the sky.

I do not know how long in the snow I wrestled
    with grisly fear;
But the stars came out and they danced about
    ere again I ventured near;
I was sick with dread, but I bravely said: 'I'll
    just take a peep inside.
I guess he's cooked, and it's time I looked';...
    then the door I opened wide.

And there sat Sam, looking cool and calm, in the
    heart of the furnace roar;
And he wore a smile you could see a mile, and
    he said: 'Please close that door.
It's fine in here, but I greatly fear you'll let in
    the cold and storm—
Since I left Plumtree, down in Tennessee, It's
    the first time I've been warm.'

There are strange things done in the midnight sun
    By men who moil for gold;
The Arctic trails have their secret tales
    That would make your blood run cold;
The Northern Lights have seen queer sights;
    But the queerest they ever did see
Was that night on the marge of Lake Le Barge
    I cremated Sam McGee.

Black Gold in the Far North

The presence of black gold—oil—on the North Slope of Alaska had been well known for at least 100 years before the Atlantic Richfield and Exxon oil companies discovered enough oil at Prudhoe Bay to make drilling commercially feasible. Because the Arctic Ocean is frozen in the winter, it was decided that a Pipeline from Prudhoe Bay south to Valdez, an all-weather port near Anchorage, was the best solution to the transportation problem. In 1970 the Alyeska Pipeline Service Company was formed to build and operate the trans-Alaska oil Pipeline, but environmentalists and special interest groups filed suit to halt the project. Three and one half years of legal and legislative battles followed, and it wasn't until 16 November 1973 that final approval was given for the Pipeline.

The environmentalist suits had accomplished one major goal: the caribou migration routes crossed the Pipeline and so Alyeska buried the pipe in a ditch so that the animals could continue in their normal habits. In this manner both sides were accommodated, perhaps not to complete satisfaction of each, but the Pipeline went through and the caribou continued to migrate. Another difficulty that required special engineering was the contraction and expansion of the pipe and the risk of earthquake damage. To allow for these possibilities, the Pipeline was designed so that between anchors it could flex up to 14 feet sideways. At the Denali Fault, an active faultline, the design permitted 20 feet of horizontal and five feet of vertical motion.

The winter of 1973-74 brought men, supplies and equipment in to build the construction camps along the Pipeline route. An enormous effort began in April 1974 to build the 360 mile road from the Yukon to Prudhoe Bay, and it took 154 days to complete the roadbed and initial gravel overlay. At the same time, work had begun on pump stations, a marine terminal and pipeline work pad and, in 1975, the first actual mainline pipe was laid into place. By the end of that year 365 miles of the 800 miles of the Pipeline already had been installed.

The Alaskan economy was booming. Wages were high and the Alaskan government was optimistic. Over 21,000 people from the standard laborers to the engineers and designers who had to plan for the smallest details, were working on the huge project.

The oil began flowing on 20 June 1977. Some construction was still going on at Pump Station 2 and 'fine tuning' of the line took over a year. Still, eventually the work was completed and those workmen not required for the continuing maintenance of the Pipeline went home. The

The fur trade also sprouted outposts, but more immediately, in the twentieth century, oil has caused many 'pipeline camps' to grow along the Alyeska Pipeline to Prudhoe Bay. Most of these camps died when the work ran out in the late 1970s. An example of such is the Chandalar Pipeline Camp *(above and at right)*, in the Brooks Range.

construction camps were abandoned to the effects of the severe weather. Little or nothing remains of them today.

Like the gold camps before them, 29 construction camps of the Pipeline were made up of men and women who had come north to make as much money as possible in a very short period of time. Yet the Pipeline workers, although similar in spirit to the eager prospectors, were in an entirely different situation. The Alyeska Pipeline Service Company hired the workers according to their own strict guidelines. Most were skilled workers—welders, fitters, plumbers and the teamsters. Unlike the prospectors, they came to Alaska, did their jobs, and most went back south to work on other construction jobs.

Below: **Isabel Pipeline Camp, at the foot of Gulkana Glacier in the Alaska Range, housed 1200 workers at its peak, and was abandoned in 1976 when the pipeline neared completion.** ***Above opposite:*** **Citizens of the Alyeska Pipeline camps when they were in full swing, during what could be called 'the Pipeline Boom.'** ***Below opposite:*** **Carpenters building a 'boom town' aka pipeline camp of the Alyeska Pipeline.**

Valdez

Valdez is at the south end of the Pipeline. The Marine Terminal, where the oil is loaded onto tankers, is located here. During the heyday of the Pipeline construction, Valdez housed over 7000 construction workers plus the hundreds of engineers, inspectors, clerks and secretaries needed to keep the project moving. Beyond these 'official' Pipeline employees there were, of course, the prostitutes and gamblers who have always gathered where money and alcohol flow. In July 1976, an Alaskan scandal centered in Valdez. Apparently six Alaskans, including two politicians, had conspired to operate a gambling and prostitution ring in the town. To be honest, the construction workers at the Terminal thought it was a pretty good idea.

Fights were as common in Valdez as they were in the old gold camps. The stress of the work, coupled with the huge variety of ethnic and ra-

cial groups, often led to misunderstandings and disagreements that erupted into battle. One fight in front of the recreation hall in August 1976 involved several Latino workers. One was a large man with a stick. He was trying to knock a knife out of a smaller man's hand when he was stabbed in the chest and arm. His girlfriend jumped in and the two of them attempted to beat the smaller man. By the time the fight was over both men were bloody and the authorities had to fly the large man to Anchorage for treatment. Meanwhile, the other workers had no idea what was happening because all the yelling was in Spanish. Rumors flew that the fight was over a debt, an unpaid loan and a pool game. No one really knew.

Another fight occurred north of Valdez, at the Livengood camp near Fairbanks. This camp was so rough that the Alaskan authorities had a trooper permanently stationed there. It seemed that a drunk Texan was busily raising hell when the trooper attempted to make the arrest in the mess hall. The other workers stood on the tables yelling, and someone threw a steak. Soon steak and potato salad were flying in every direction. The Texan had a lot of friends and they all jumped into the fight. Before it was over more troopers had arrived and the two ringleaders of the riot were arrested. Ironically, the Texan got away. Although this fight made the front page of the Valdez newspaper, most fights along the Pipeline were quick and personal.

Alcohol was a constant problem. In *Crazy Money* by Potter Wickware, Potter tells of one bender that he and his friends went on in Valdez. Drinks were flowing and the men were buying for people they didn't even know. This was called six-packing—only the six-packs were 100 proof. The last thing Potter remembers of that night was three six-packs, or 18 bourbon and waters, lined up on the table in front of him. His friends later told him that they all stumbled out to catch the bus back to camp at 3 o'clock in the morning. The late bus stopped across the highway, past a rockpile. The group fell down and groped their way over the rockpile and couldn't find the bus stop! It was raining heavily

and when they finally did find the stop, the red taillights of the bus glowed at them as it pulled away. Potter fell into a mudhole and lost his glasses before the group broke into a shack. They waited there for the four o'clock bus, laughing and talking. Alcohol had made them all friends. There was no mention of any friendships the next morning. Hangovers being the ugly creatures that they are, it is not surprising that Potter did not reflect on his 'morning after.'

Humor along the Pipeline was rough. Unprintable stories abounded, yet there were some that could be repeated. One story, sensitive to the workers' situation of work, stress, alcohol and lack of feminine companionship told of how one man went nuts in camp. His fellow workers found him naked in the parking lot, with a strange expression on his face. He had a chain of beer cans tied around his neck. When asked, 'What are you doing?' he replied, 'I'm going upstream to spawn.'

Insanity was not exclusive to the Pipeline workers alone. In Joe McGinniss' book, *Going to Extremes*, he writes of an incident at the Valdez travel agency. As Joe was speaking to the manager, a young woman with two deep scars across her face came into the office. She wanted to see the manager immediately. He tried to put her off. She didn't move. She reached into her handbag and pulled out a .357 Magnum. She didn't say anything, just stood there, her whole body trembling. She and the manager stepped out of the office. The manager then returned, explaining to Joe that the lady was once a first class prostitute in town. She had a bad accident and with the scars on her face, she was no longer number one, so she began running cocaine in from New York. On her last trip she'd managed to lose the coke and now had three

Below: **Plastic is good weatherproofing, as this scene evidences.** ***Above:*** **Construction at a pipeline camp.** ***Above right, both:*** **Valdez, Alaska is the pipeline's marine terminal. Valdez pre-existed the pipeline, and has the northernmost ice-free harbor in the USA.** ***Below right:*** **The Five Mile Pipeline Camp.**

days to get the $20,000 to cover the loss of the drug or her 'boss' was going to make her facial scars the least of her worries.

As the manager hustled out of his office with a couple of blank ticket forms, he said that he'd be out of the office for awhile. The lady wanted $500 in cash and a one-way ticket to San Francisco. The manager was going to take care of her 'problem' before she did something foolish.

'Wow,' he said when leaving. 'I bet this kind of shit doesn't happen in Saudi Arabia!'

Valdez was a small town before the Pipeline came and, with the construction completed, the workers went home, leaving the town with only 3000 inhabitants. Compared to the days of the Pipeline construction, Valdez again became a sleepy village on the Alaskan coastline.

Prudhoe Bay

Between Valdez and Prudhoe Bay stretches the entire 798 miles of the Alaskan Pipeline. The pumping stations, a half a dozen towns and the city of Fairbanks are the only permanent settlements on the James Dalton Highway. The construction camps have deteriorated since the Pipeline was completed. The extreme cold at Prudhoe Bay and Deadhorse caused many difficulties that the workers at Valdez didn't have to worry about. In the cold and low humidity, garbage would not decompose, machinery would not rust. The men could not work quickly, nor would they want to. If they breathed too quickly, the air itself could kill them—frosted lungs. There were no small mistakes. There was a story that circulated about a soldier on maneuvers outside of Fairbanks. He had brought along a flask to 'keep himself warm.' He took one gulp in the -50 degree weather and dropped dead, his throat frozen closed. The alcohol would not freeze but the liquid was -50 degrees when it entered his throat. It certainly didn't warm him!

Below: The makings of a pipeline camp. _Opposite: above left,_ everyday work at a pipeline camp; and _above right,_ a bear comes to investigate. _Opposite, below:_ Tonsina, Alaska. _Overleaf:_ An early settler's cabin on Afognak Island, Alaska.

In those extreme conditions even the presence of men seemed bizarre. The buildings, the machinery, even the men were alien to the land. Yet they came, did their jobs and left. When the equipment was first brought north in August 1974, nature played one of its nastier tricks on ARCO. The ice pack moves offshore for about six weeks of every year and barges could be brought through, carrying millions of dollars worth of pipe and other equipment. Prudhoe Bay remains on the North Slope, pumping oil to be sent southward to the waiting tankers at the Main Terminal. Unexpectedly, the ice pack moved back in to shore and the barges were frozen in for the winter. They could not be moved until July so trucks had to be driven out onto the ice to unload supplies. For those months the barges were like ghost ships. Papers were left on desks, coffee was still frozen in the paper cups. The barges were an amazing contrast to the well-lit and heated quarters of the workers. Yet it was here, in Prudhoe Bay, where the construction workers rioted in the dining hall when they were informed that steak and lobster would be served on alternate nights instead of at the same meal. Perhaps this seems unreasonable, considering that the men made up to $2000 a week, plus room and board. Still, with working conditions of -50 degrees and twelve-hour shifts, maybe the men deserved their steak and lobster at every meal.

Today, the massive job of building the Pipeline is complete and the workers have gone home to the lower 48 states. A few fell in love with Alaska and stayed, trying to make a living in the local businesses and industries.

Still, the North Slope Haul Road remains, now renamed the James Dalton Highway. Along this road the pump stations and Pipeline can be viewed and, here and there along the line, there is access to such old mining towns as Coldfoot at State Creek and Wiseman.

The oil of Prudhoe Bay and Kuparuk is expected to last until sometime into the early 21st century. Prospects of new oil discoveries remain and the possibility of extending the Pipeline is a viable option. Still, should the oil run out, the Pipeline, the pumping stations and the two terminals could become the new ghost towns of the Far North.

Whispers in the Wind

Today, the wealth of precious metals that brought prospectors to the West has largely been extracted and the mines are closed, but the fascination with the towns and folklore they created is ongoing. The lure of gold still pulls men into the mountains and deserts to search for elusive riches. As the value of the dollar drops, the price of gold goes up and the prospectors load up their pickups with supplies and head back out to the old claims. Hope never dies in the miner's heart. All it will take is one more shovelful, one more winter's rain, one more rock accidentally kicked over, and the new rush will begin.

Even as new ghost towns are born, some old towns are revitalized. Places like Calico, California and Cripple Creek, Colorado have become part of a new industry: tourism. Old legends are resurrected by historians and public relations firms alike. The ruins of towns like Bodie, California are being preserved for posterity. Thus, the wind still whistles through the abandoned buildings and moans among the surrounding hills. No matter how many years pass, the great-great-grandchildren of America's pioneers can come, sit among the battered houses, and listen for the voices of the past, the whispers of the wind.

Perhaps Walter Noble Burns captured this emotion best in concluding his book *Tombstone*. The story never ends, only the people and the locations change:

Below: **Mogollon, New Mexico. Once a booming gold town, Mogollon is now virtually deserted. It's eight miles east of Alma, on State Route 78.** ***At right:*** **The old Cochise County courthouse in Tombstone, Arizona, 'The town too tough to die.'**

COCHISE
COUNTY

'...when a coyote lifts a weird song in the mesquite and moon hangs over the Dragoons, it is easy to imagine it the frontier boulevard it used to be. Then the disfiguring scars left by the years disappear, and the ancient buildings, bathed in the soft light as in a fountain of youth, seem clothed in the strength and freshness of old days. The present fades; the past rises like a picture. There in the street are the lumber trains coming in from the Chiricahuas; the sixteen-mule ore teams with their clanking trace chains; the yells of mule-skinners, the cracking of whips. The arcaded sidewalks are crowded. Swing doors of saloons flail back and forth. Laughter of roistering throngs comes from the brightly lighted bars. You hear the click of faro chips, the rattle of roulette wheels. The scent of spiced drinks and orange peel is in the air. That tall man there with the six-shooters buckled around him is Wyatt Earp. Doc Holliday is lounging in a doorway. Yonder are Virgil and Morgan Earp. Johnny Behan bustles along. And the Clantons and McLowerys and Buckskin Frank and John Ringo in his great buffalo coat, his hands rammed in his pockets on his guns. And Curly Bill and his bold buccaneers, riding in from the San Simon, go clattering past...when a coyote lifts a weird song in the mesquite and the moon hangs over the Dragoons.

'Tombstone flames no more. Its wild days are a tale that is told. It lives with its memories and its ghosts. Sunshine and peace are its portion. Once it was romance. Now it's a town.'

Below: **Memorial to a ghost town life, in Mariposa, California.** ***At right:*** **The sun beats down upon the weathered remains of Bodie, California.** ***Overleaf:*** **Sun-bleached boards invite the inquiring mind to the ghost town of Congress, Arizona.**

GLOSSARY

adobe: sun-dried brick; the mixed earth or clay used to make such bricks.

arrastres: Spanish name for the primitive quartz mills or ore-crushers first used in the California Gold Rush.

assay: to test ores or minerals by chemical or furnace examination; gold and silver require an additional process called 'cupelling' to separate them from the base metals.

bar: accumulation of sand and gravel along the banks of a stream, which are worked by the placer miners for gold; then they are called bar diggings.

basin: a large or small depression of the surface of the land, the lowest part of which may be occupied by a lake or pond.

bedrock: the solid rock underlying gravel, sand, and clay deposits.

bonanza: in miners' phrase, good luck, or a body of rich ore; a mine is in bonanza when it is highly profitable.

Chilean War: altercation near Mokelumne Hill, California, between Chilean and American miners.

claim: the portion of mining ground held under the federal and local laws by one claimant or association; the portion of land within a mining district to which a miner is entitled.

color: the shade or tint of the earth or rock which indicates ore; also, a particle or particles of metallic gold found in the prospector's pan after a sample of earth or crushed rock has been 'panned out.'

cyanide process: the extraction of gold from finely crushed ores, concentrates, and tailings by means of cyanide of potassium in diluted solutions; the gold is dissolved by the solution and subsequently deposited upon metallic zinc; often coated with mercury.

diggings: applicable to all mineral deposits and mining camps, but in common usage in the United States applied to placer mining only.

dredge: a scoop or suction apparatus, operated by power, and usually mounted on a flat-bottomed boat; extensively used in mining gold-bearing sand and gravel.

drift: a horizontal passage underground which follows a vein, as distinguished from a 'crosscut' which intersects a vein of ore.

fault: a break in the continuity of a body of rock, associated with some movement on one side or the other of the break, so that what were once parts of one continuous rock stratum or vein are now separated.

float: pieces of ore or rock which have fallen from veins or strata, or have been separated from the parent vein or strata by natural weathering.

flume: an inclined channel usually of wood and often supported on a trestle,used to convey water for power, transportation, and washing; commonly used in placer mining, logging, and irrigation.

galena: the commonest lead mineral; shiny gray in color.

ghost town: according to Webster's, a town, especially a Western boom town, that has been totally abandoned. For the purposes of this book, I have modified the definition to include towns that are but a faded remnant of their former selves since most of the completely abandoned towns have completely disappeared (except in the deserts of the Southwest).

gold dust: fine particles of gold.

gold pan: round pan used to swirl gravel and water together until the lighter rocks have sloshed out, leaving the heavier gold in the bottom of the pan.

grubstakes: supplies furnished to a prospector on the promise of a share in his discoveries; so called because the lender stakes or risks the grub on the chances of the prospector.

Hangtown: now known as Placerville, California; the town got its name for hosting the first recorded lynching in the Mother Lode.

Hangtown Fry: a fried mixture of eggs, oysters, bacon and other greasy ingredients; originated in Hangtown, now known as Placerville.

horn silver: chloride of silver.

hydraulic mining: a method of mining in which a bank of gold-bearing earth or gravel is washed away by powerful jets of water.

hydraulicking: washing down a bank of earth or gravel by the use of water under high pressure.

Klondike: a region in Canada's Yukon Territory, originally the mispronunciation of an Indian word 'Trundeck;' Trundeck was their name for a stream later known by white traders as Deer Creek.

lode: strictly a fissure in the country rock filled with some mineral.

mill: any establishment for reducing ores by any means other than smelting.

mill site: a plot of ground suitable for the erection of a mill, or reduction works; used in connection with mining operations.

mining district: a section of country, usually designated by name and described or understood as being confined within certain natural boundaries, in which valuable minerals may be found in paying quantities.

Mother Lode: the principal lode or vein of rich ore passing through a district or particular section of the country.

placer: a place where gold is obtained by washing; an alluvial or glacial deposit of sand or gravel, containing particles of gold or other valuable minerals.

placer mining: usually refers to panning or rocking for gold.

pocket mining: digging small 'pockets' of gold out of hillsides and either hauling water up or the gravel down to the stream and panning it for gold.

quartz mining: the gold-bearing quartz had to be dug out from the surrounding rock before it could be crushed and the gold separated out; often the shafts went down hundreds of feet; the first mines to make deep shaft mining profitable were the Kennedy and Argonaut in Jackson, California.

sink: any slight depression in the land surface, especially one having no outlet.

smelting works: an establishment in which metals are extracted from their ores by furnaces.

stamp mill: the building or apparatus in which rock is crushed by descending pestles (stamps) operated by water or steam-power.

tailings: the worthless slimes left behind after the valuable portion of the ore has been separated by some form of concentration.

telluride: a compound of tellurium which is often rich in gold and silver.

wire silver: native silver in the form of wire or threads.

Yukon: a territory in northwestern Canada adjacent to Alaska; also the name of a river that flows out of Canada and across Alaska, Yukon was originally the Athabascan word for 'clear waters' which the Indians called the headwaters of the present day Yukon River.

These pages, clockwise from above: **The historical site of Columbia, California; a Montana ghost town; a gold stream, almost dry in the summer; a nineteenth century medical kit, replete with strychnine and novocaine, on display in Columbia; the ghost town of Humphrey, Idaho; and the aptly-named Apacheland 'ghost mine' in Arizona.**

Index

Acknowledgments

I would like to thank Bill Yenne for giving me this opportunity; Timothy Jacobs, Pam Berkman, Tom Debolski, and my parents, Don and Hazel Griffith for all of their support and encouragement; and last but not least, Bison Books, for making this whole project possible. Many states contributed wonderful photos and reference materials for this book and I appreciate their help. Invaluable reference sources included *Ghost Towns of the American West* by Robert Silverberg; *Ghost Town El Dorado* and *Ghost Towns of the West* by Lambert Florin; *Gold is the Cornerstone* by John Walton Caughey; *Ghost Towns and Mining Camps of California* by Remi A Nadeau; and other materials from the early 20th century that are too numerous to mention.

Photo Credits

Alaska Division of Tourism 177 (top and bottom right), 178–179, 181, 182–183, 184–185
Joel Bennett 196–197
Alyeska Pipeline Service Company 188, 189, 190–191 (bottom), 192 (all), 193 (top left and bottom)
George Herben/Alaska Photo 193 (top right)
Clark Mishler 191 (top)
Nancy Simmerman/Alaska Photo 195 (top right)
© American Graphic Systems 37, 59
American Graphic Systems Archives 10, 13, 34–35, 60 (top), 65 (top), 162 (all), 164 (top left and right), 165 (top), 169 (top right), 172 (top), 173 (bottom)
Orville Andrews 2–3, 30, 103, 121 (bottom), 122–123 (all), 124, 200–201
Arizona Office of Tourism 125 (top), 126, 127 (bottom), 128, 129 (bottom), 169 (top left), 199, 202–203, 205 (top right)
Burlington Northern 158
California Department of Parks and Recreation 25 (top)
California State Library 4–5, 24, 25 (bottom), 26–27, 34, 35, 38, 39, 46–47, 49 (bottom), 52, 54 (top), 56, 61 (all), 64, 65 (bottom), 75 (bottom), 76–77 (all), 83 (top), 88 (all), 96, 97, 98–99, 100, 101, 102, 104–105, 106–107 (all), 108 (all), 110, 111 (all), 113, 114–115, 120 (bottom), 131 (top)
John Campo 71 (bottom left and right), 169 (bottom)
Cinema Shop 119, 129 (top), 148 (top and bottom right)
Dahlonega Gold Museum, Georgia 19, 20 (all), 21 (all), 132 (all)
© RE DeJauregui 6, 42 (all), 43 (all), 44 (all), 45, 49 (top), 60 (bottom), 78–79, 81 (all), 84 (all), 85 (all), 86 (all), 87 (all), 89, 90 (all), 91 (all), 92 (all), 93 (all), 200, 208
Denver Public Library, Western History Department 133, 134, 135 (all), 136 (all), 137 (all), 138–139, 140–141, 142–143, 144, 154 (top), 157 (bottom)
Kentucky Department of Travel Development 11, 14–15
J&J Kidd 131
© KD Kirkland 145, 155 (top right and bottom), 205 (left)
Las Vegas News Bureau 163, 166, 168
The Reverend MJ McPike Collection 152 (bottom left and right), 157 (top), 175
Mississippi Department of Economic Development 7
Montana Travel Promotion Bureau 8–9, 153
Harley Hettick 156
Gary Wunderwald 154 (bottom), 155 (top left), 204 (bottom right)
National Archives 149
Nebraska Department of Economic Development 31 (all), 33
New Mexico Economic Development and Tourism Department 130–131, 198
Oklahoma Tourism
Fred W Marvel 18
William M Robblee 118–119
San Francisco Presidio Museum 28
Seaver Center for Western History Research, Natural History Museum of Los Angeles County 22, 23, 36 (bottom), 40, 80–81, 94–95, 109, 112, 116–117, 118, 125 (bottom), 150–151, 161 (top), 164–165, 166–167, 173 (top), 176–177
South Dakota Tourism
Mark Kayser 148 (bottom left)
Southern Pacific 32–33, 159, 160–161 (bottom)
© W Thomas Tizard 1, 127 (top left and right), 129 (top), 170, 171 (all), 172 (bottom)
Tourism Canada
Bob Anderson 186 (bottom)
Mike Beedel 187
Drie/Meir 186 (top)
Bill McLeod 180
Virginia Division of Tourism 16
Wyoming Travel Commission 146, 147 (all)
© Bill Yenne 17, 29, 36 (top), 41 (both), 48, 50–51 (all), 53, 54 (bottom), 70, 71 (top), 72–73, 74, 75 (top), 82, 83 (bottom), 152 (top), 204 (left and top right), 205 (bottom)

Overleaf: **Downieville, California. It's like stepping back through the years, but for the far-off whine of a jet flying over. The old honky tonk saloon down the street may no longer overflow with miners, but the reminiscence lives on.**